POOR NO MORE

KERVIN J. SMITH

rill &
associates

Poor No More, I'm Making The Switch To Rich

ISBN: 978-0-9832536-6-2

Printed in the United States of America.

Rill & Associates
P.O. Box 119, Orrstown, PA 17244
303.503.7257; Fax: 717.477.2261

1 2 3 4 5 6 7 / 15 14 13

SPECIAL THANKS

I appreciate and respect every one of you in whatever capacity of ministry you serve in. Your position in the five-fold ministry of the church is crucial and paramount in these last days. God bless you, and I love you.

Funmilayo Aimila
Minister Esther Ajiboye
Pastor Wale Ajiboye
Sherifat Alabi
Pinky Alexander
Tameka Alicea
Andre Channer-Allen
Ida Alston
Lila Alvarado
Shay Atkins
Dedra Bailey
Jannet Barnes
Sonia Batson
Owen Baxter
Cassandra Blissett
Sandra Bolden
LaRosa BoltonNathaniel
Bonaparte Jr.
Bishop Patricia Broadney
Novlette Brown
Clapieese Buchanan

Ruby Buggs
Orsia Kelly-Burke
Janice P. Cammon
Donald & Renee Campbell
Shirley Channer
David Clarke
Judith Rosemay Clarke
Sister Clarke
Marjorie Cole
Earnestine Coles
Joseph Collins
Sylather Collins
Tracey-Ann Collins
Veronica Coomber
Dr. Candace L. Cooper
Mozet Corley
Yvonne Davis
Lenett Casey-Destor
Zelma DeVeaux
Kathy Dix
Yvonne Dottin

Samuel Duncan
Gregory Duhavey
Alfreda Dunlap
Grace Duru
Nigel & Desreen Dyer
Natasha Elliott
Nwabueze Titus Eze
Jackie Ford
Bereeta Foster
Mia Freeman
Sharon Frye
Gwendolyn Gantt
Valarie Golding
Margaret Gydoi
Everette Haughton
NaCosha M. Hayes
Patricia Hazelwood
Helen Hewitt
Sabrina Hicks
Terry Hicks
Rose-Marie Hill
Robert & Juliet Hollin
Betty Holmes
Timothy & Stacey Hunter
Mr. & Mrs. Huntley
Rita Inyang
Denise Jackson
Tockie Jackson
Renee Jackson

Stacey Jenkins
Elaine Johnson
Georgetta Johnson
Geraldine Johnson
Winsome Johnson
Pat Jones
Joanna Joseph
Pastor Deborah Kargbo
June & Radcliffe Kelly
Christal Kerr
Gloria King
Brenda Kingston
Cheri Kingston
Doreen Leach
James & Patricia Lemon
Antoinettte Lewis
Cathy Mack
Jer'Quille Mack
Wendy Mahoney
Elvina Malone
Shaun Manuel
Beverly Marghal
Lloyd McCray
Delores McLean
David & Jennifer Metelus
Vernon Milk
Ann Marie Miller
Claudette Miller
Debra Miller

Joan Miller
Ian Miller
Maxine Miller
Sadie Miller
LaGina Moncrief
Temeko Moore
Faith Morris
Lenett Casey-Nestor
Ronell Casey-Nestor
Lucy Ngebeh
Deswaine Norton
Patience Ogbebor
Pastor James Ogundare
Ibironke Ogunye
Lola Olanrewaju
Rev. & Mrs. Olanrewaju
Janis Wafer Overton
Carmen Peart
Patricia Perez
Bishop Milton B. Perry
Nancy Person
Sonia Person
Minister Martha Pollett
Mark Powel
Javonna Richardson
Diane Robinson
Acie & Angela V. Sanders

Jacquelyn Seibles
Theresa Shepard
Claudette Skerritt
Veronica Simpson
Lorraine Smith
Octavia Smith
Patricia Sparks
Michael Stanford
Timothy Stephenson
Diane Stewart
Connie Tate
Ingrid Taylor
Chanelle Thompson
Deidra Thrift
Kim Titus
Angellina Tshuma
Karen Tucker
Tina Unuigbe
Betty Vereen
Abie Viassy
Jessica Wade
Pastors Johnnie & Cindy White
Bishop Theotis White
Ann-Marie Williams
Donna Williams
Harlene Wilson
Ashley Wright

Do not fret because of evildoers, nor be envious of the workers of iniquity. For they shall soon be cut down like the grass, and wither as the green herb. Trust in the Lord, and do good; dwell in the land, and feed on His faithfulness. Delight yourself also in the Lord, and He shall give you the desires of your heart. Commit your way to the Lord, trust also in Him, and He shall bring it to pass. He shall bring forth your righteousness as the light, and your justice as the noonday. **Rest in the Lord, and wait patiently for Him; do not fret because of him who prospers in his way, because of the man who brings wicked schemes to pass**

PSALM 37:1-7

TABLE OF CONTENTS

Chapter One

WHO DO YOU TRUST?

Today in America we are in the worst financial and economic crisis that our country has faced in at least a generation. Unemployment nationwide has reached a level unseen since the 1970s—and stubbornly refuses to come down. The U.S. economy is sluggish at best; gasoline prices are way up and the value of the dollar is way down. Public confidence in the economy has dropped as well. Millions of American households are reeling from the repeated one-two punches of a stubborn recession and high unemployment. An ongoing housing crisis of unprecedented proportions makes the situation even worse. Over the past two or three years hundreds of thousands of American homeowners have faced foreclosure and the subsequent destruction of their "American dream." Many of these homeowners, unable to meet their monthly house payments, have simply walked away from their homes—and their mortgages. Hardworking Americans at every level are losing their homes, jobs, investments, life savings, and sometimes even their health. Worst of all, many are losing hope. For them, the American dream of prosperity and home ownership has become a nightmare of uncertainty, insecurity, and fear.

Much of the uncertainty is due to the difficulty in correctly identifying the problem. Economic "experts" differ over not only the nature and scope of the problem but also over the nature of the solution. Some say that stimulus payments and bailouts are the answer; others insist that those "solutions" only make the problem worse. Some declare that more government spending is needed; others are just as adamant that spending cuts are the only way to go. Some blame the problem on the greed of bankers, brokers, and the business sector in general; others say that flawed economic policy, poor judgment, and bad decisions are to blame.

There are many seeds that gave rise to the present crisis, but one thing that seems clear to most analysts is that our current economic difficulties stem in large part from a banking crisis linked to a near collapse in the housing market.

THE RISE AND DEMISE

The first half of the first decade of the 21st century witnessed a housing boom in America as the federal government, in a well-intentioned but ill-conceived effort to make home ownership available to a wider spectrum of Americans, pressured banks, credit unions, and other lending organizations to ease their restrictions on mortgage approvals to make them more affordable and easier to obtain for more Americans. Consequently, financial institutions concocted new and different strategies and loan programs, such as subprime mortgages, interest-only loans, "jumbo" loans, and nothing down, 100% financed mortgages. Many of these "affordable" options incorporated variable interest rates as opposed to fixed rates. Under this arrangement, a very low interest rate, and therefore a low monthly payment, would be locked in for the first several years of the mortgage. After that initial locked-in period, the interest rate (and the monthly payment) would rise to reflect the current prime rate.

At first this effort to increase the number of Americans who owned their own home seemed to work. Mortgage approvals increased substantially, as did the number of first-time homeowners. The downside, however, was that these relaxed standards resulted in mortgage approvals being given to many people who never would have qualified otherwise, either because of insufficient income or some other reason. But when the low initial rates period ended and the higher interest rates kicked in, many of these mortgage holders suddenly found themselves saddled with high monthly payments that they simply could not afford. Homeowners by the thousands began defaulting on their mortgages, and their homes went into foreclosure. There were so many foreclosures at one time that lending institutions nationwide suffered massive losses. The sudden glut of foreclosed houses available on the market, combined with the declining value of the dollar and other depressive effects of an economic downturn, caused property values in general to plummet. In many cases, even homeowners who were still able to manage their monthly house payments discovered that they owed more in mortgage debt than their house was worth.

As a result of these record losses in the banking industry, the credit markets froze. Whenever the credit markets freeze, spending always slows down, demands for goods and services decrease, production decreases, profits decrease, and the stock market slows down. The United States went into a recession. Many businesses began to struggle financially, and in order to survive were forced to cut their losses. Employees were laid off, and the unemployment rolls began to grow. Adding to the problem, thousands of new college graduates joined the ranks of the unemployed as they found employment hard to come by or even nonexistent in an increasingly anemic job market.

Who is responsible for this mess? Many blame it on unsound government economic policies and runaway spending, while others say that corporate greed and irresponsible behavior are responsible. Undoubtedly, all of these play a part, but responsibility extends much further. To one degree or another, *responsibility for our economic problems lies with all of us.* We have bought into a consumer-driven, instant gratification, get-rich-quick mentality that insists that we have to have everything we want right now. We are always seeking "easy street." The corporate world feeds this mentality by offering us easy credit and time payments so we can satisfy our every desire with the simple swipe of a plastic card.

Businesses and financial institutions dangle carrots of greater revenues in front of us with the claim that quick financial gains may be ours. With the promise of easy money they play upon the greed, gullibility, and financial ignorance of consumers. It should come as no surprise then that one of the biggest financial traps that Americans fall into is the credit trap. In the interest of making a fast buck and trying to get ahead quickly, many people have built their financial foundation

RESPONSIBILITY FOR OUR ECONOMIC PROBLEMS LIES WITH ALL OF US.

on deception, inexperienced trading, tips from unlicensed brokers or journalists on their favorite cable network, or some get-rich-quick tip they heard from their barber or their beautician. They have bought homes they cannot afford and cars they don't need and have leveraged themselves to the hilt, all because the powers that be in the corporate and financial worlds have said, "You need this, you deserve this, and you can have it *now*."

Consumer confidence is low and many Americans are afraid for their financial future. "Will I lose my job?"

(Or if currently unemployed), "When will I find a job?" "Will I lose my house?" "Will I be able to make the car payment this month?" "Will I be able to feed my family?" "What if one of the kids gets sick?" "What's going to happen to my pension?" Many Americans have had the foundation of their lives thoroughly shaken and don't know where to turn. In these times of uncertainty and instability, where can we find a safe haven? Is there such a place? Let me make it personal: When things seem to be falling apart around you, where can you turn for peace of mind, confidence, and prosperity? To put it another way, *who do you trust with your future?*

Do you trust the federal government? You shouldn't; not in the face of $14 trillion of debt, out-of-control spending, and burdensome taxes on the people that threaten to get worse.

Do you trust your bank account, pension plan, or 401(k)? Bad idea. Banks can fail (and many have during this crisis). Many employers, feeling the relentless squeeze of financial pressures, are being forced to downsize and streamline their organizations, which for some means cutting back on their pension plan or 401(k), or even eliminating it altogether.

Do you trust your investments? Too risky. While informed investing in the stock market is a wise financial move, it is unwise to depend on those investments for your security or to stake your life on the expectation of receiving positive returns from them or any other financial vehicle.

Money, when understood and used properly, and when kept in its proper place, can be a blessing and an instrument of great good, but it is not a suitable foundation upon which to build one's life. The apostle Paul had this to say about money: *"For the love of money is the root of all evil: which while some coveted after, they have erred from the faith, and pierced themselves through with many sorrows"* (1 Tim. 6:10 KJV). Notice that Paul does not say that *money* is a root of evil, but the *love* of money. And even the word *love* needs more explanation because the English word does not capture the full meaning of the original Greek. In Greek, the word Paul uses for "love" here is *philagyria*. Appearing here only in the New Testament, *philagyria* literally means "covetousness" or "avarice." So it is not mere affection for money that is a root of evil, Paul says, but a covetous attitude toward money. Everyone likes money and everyone needs money, and as long as we keep our priorities straight about money, there is no problem. But to become obsessed with money and its acquisition; to be preoccupied with money every waking moment; to live for money—this is what leads to evil.

So where do we place our trust? Can we prosper and live in peace and confidence and security in the midst of uncertain times? Yes, but only if our eyes are focused on the right source. And that calls for discernment. We need to know the source of our security, and we need to understand the times in which we live. We need to be like the sons of Issachar, *"who had understanding of the times, to know what Israel ought to do"* (1 Chron. 12:32a).

THE ONLY TRUSTWORTHY SOURCE

There is only one source worthy of our trust, whether in financial matters or any other arena of life: We must trust in the Lord. He alone is the true source of our peace, security, and prosperity. Consider the words of King David of Israel:

Trust in the Lord, and do good; dwell in the land, and feed on His faithfulness. Delight yourself also in the Lord, and He shall give you the desires of your heart. Commit your way to the Lord, trust also in Him, and He shall bring it to pass. He shall bring forth your righteousness as the light, and your justice as the noonday. Rest in the Lord, and wait patiently for Him (Psalm 37:3-7a).

In these verses David gives us four instructions that clearly show us where we should place our trust. The last three build on and expand the first one, which is the key to everything else.

First of all, David tells us to *"trust in the Lord, and do good; dwell in the land, and feed on His faithfulness."* The Hebrew word for "trust" here is *batach,* which means to rely on and depend on with complete confidence. To trust in this sense means to depend utterly on someone else to support you, to hold you up when you cannot support yourself. Think of it this way. If you are hiking up a mountain and sprain your ankle, the only way you're going to get back down is if you have someone to lean on, someone you can depend on in complete confidence to get you safely to the bottom.

So what David is saying here is that we are to "lean on" God. When things get tough, lean on God. When the economy takes a tumble, lean on God. When troubles beset you left and right, lean on God. Don't lean on your job, or your 401(k), or your investments; your faith is not built on these. Your faith is built on God, so lean on Him. If you trust in the Lord, if you lean on God, He will move you and take you to places beyond your wildest dreams. But it begins with trust: complete and utter dependence on God and an absolute confidence that He will build you up and prosper you for your good and His glory.

The second phrase of verse 3 elaborates on the first: *"Dwell in the land, and feed on His faithfulness."* In this case the Hebrew word for "dwell," *shakan*, carries the idea of settling down permanently. It means that our trust in the Lord is so complete and our confidence in Him so absolute, that we can relax wherever we are, in whatever circumstances,

WHEN THINGS GET TOUGH, LEAN ON GOD.

and know that we are perfectly safe in Him. When we trust in the Lord, we depend on His faithfulness for our "food"— everything that we need to sustain life. That means we don't trust in our bank account but in His faithfulness. We don't trust in our 401(k) or pension plan but in His faithfulness. We don't trust in our own knowledge or abilities, but in His faithfulness to provide.

David's second instruction to us is, *"Delight yourself also in the Lord, and He shall give you the desires of your heart."* To delight means to take pleasure in, to enjoy, to experience happiness. In other words, be happy in the Lord, and He shall give you the desires of your heart. I don't care what's going on around you; I don't care what circumstances you are in. I don't care if you've been pushed down more times than you can count; get up and be happy in the Lord, knowing that there is going to be a brighter day, a better tomorrow, because God is going to turn your situation around. And when you delight yourself in the Lord, you quickly discover that He is your greatest delight, and therefore the greatest desire of your heart.

BE HAPPY IN THE LORD.

In this case, the word *Lord* actually refers to God's personal, covenant-keeping, contractual name, Jehovah. Who is Jehovah? He is whoever you need Him to be; when you need Him to be it. If you are broke, He becomes Jehovah-Jireh, the God who provides. If you are sick, He becomes Jehovah-Rophe, the God who heals. If you have hell or pandemonium going on in your life, He becomes Jehovah-Shalom, the God of peace. When you trust in the Lord and delight yourself in Him, He becomes whoever you need Him to be, regardless of your circumstances, because He is all-sufficient, able to supply your every need. God is saying to each of us, "Be happy in Me because you have a covenant. Be happy in Me because you have a contract." The moment you were born again through faith in Jesus Christ as your Lord and Savior, you came into covenant with Almighty God. So what are you worried about? It doesn't matter what the economy is doing or what the chairman of the Federal Reserves has to say. All you need to know is that God is with you and will provide for you. He will never leave you or forsake you.

The third instruction that David gives us is this: *"Commit your way to the Lord, trust also in Him, and He shall bring it to pass."* To commit literally means "to roll off the burdens." God wants us to roll all of our burdens onto His shoulders: every care, every concern, every fear, every worry, every hope, every dream, every aspiration. When we trust Him with these things, He takes care of them—every one.

Please understand, however, that God does not make our load light so that we can relax and become irresponsible. He does it so that our lives can be balanced. One of the many tasks that the captain of an airliner is responsible for is making sure the aircraft is not overweight or out of balance. There are certain gauges aboard the aircraft that the pilot looks at to make sure everything is balanced. Every so often a flight attendant may approach a passenger and say, "Sir, would you please come sit up front," because they are trying to balance the aircraft. That's what God is saying to each of us. He wants you to be balanced. He wants you to commit yourself so that you can serve Him better. In other words, you have to be balanced to the point where you are not veering off to the left or to the right but staying on course, always knowing what God is saying.

David's fourth instruction, in verse 7, is, *"Rest in the Lord, and wait patiently for Him."* The Hebrew word for "rest" literally means to be silent, to be still, to hold one's peace, to quiet oneself, to display an absolute confidence and calmness in the things of God.

We all need to take time to rest in the Lord and bask in His presence. This means stilling our minds and becoming quiet. The problem is that many people today hate silence. Silence makes many of us uncomfortable because silence always makes us responsible. What's the first thing most of us do when we get in the car? Turn on the radio. What's one of the first things we do when we get home? Turn on the television or play some music. We have noise over here, noise over there, and we try to keep ourselves busy with something. We often feel uncomfortable with silence because silence makes us think. The moment things get quiet is the moment all the unpleasant and unwanted thoughts intrude—all the self-doubt, self-condemnation, fear, and insecurity that we have been able to keep at bay by surrounding ourselves with a busy and noisy environment.

> BE
> BALANCED.

Silence makes us do a self-examination. It makes us look introspectively at ourselves. Silence forces us to make decisions we have been postponing. We may call our busyness "multitasking," but the truth of the matter is that there are certain areas of our lives that we don't want God to shine His light on.

We need to learn to rest in the Lord because when we do not rest in Him, we rob ourselves of one of His greatest gifts to us: a peaceful heart.

No matter what your circumstances, no matter where you stand in the current economic crisis, take heart, for God wants you to be *poor no more*. It has nothing to do with the economy, but everything to do with His promises and His faithfulness.

So who do you trust? If you trust in the government, or the banks, or the markets, or any of the things or institutions of this world, you will be continually disappointed and your days will be filled with uncertainty, insecurity, and fear.

There is a better way. Trust in the Lord and depend on His faithfulness. Delight yourself in the Lord and let Him fulfill your heart's desire. Commit your way to the Lord and

REST IN THE LORD.

let Him prepare you, position you, and advance you in His good time. Rest in the Lord; let Him become for you

25

Jehovah-Shalom, the God of peace, who gives you peace in the midst of a world of turmoil.

> *Be anxious for nothing, but in everything by prayer and supplication, with thanksgiving, let your requests be made known to God; and the peace of God, which surpasses all understanding, will guard your hearts and minds through Christ Jesus* (Philippians 4:6-7).

Chapter Two

WHAT'S IN YOUR HAND?

In our current economic climate it seems as though the idea of a "bailout" is on everybody's mind. And why not? After all, over the last two or three years we've seen government bailouts of car companies (GM and Chrysler), insurance companies (AIG), banks and other financial institutions (Merrill-Lynch, Goldman-Sachs, Lehman Brothers), and several other businesses that were deemed by the government as "too big to fail." On a related issue, hundreds of businesses nationwide have applied for and received waivers allowing them temporarily to opt out of the requirements of the new health care law because those requirements are too costly for them to bear.

The American public by and large has been divided over this issue of bailouts and waivers. Some say they are necessary to keep our economy afloat while others insist that they do nothing to solve the underlying problem, which is massive debt and overspending. Many struggling taxpayers, weary from trying to meet house payments and other basic expenses during difficult times, have called out cynically to the powers that be in Washington, "Where's *my* bailout? Where's *my* waiver?"

Whatever your personal take on the wisdom or fairness of the government bailouts, it is important to understand that a bailout, essentially, is a temporary solution delaying the inevitable. Think of trying to cross a lake in a leaky boat. Water enters the bottom of the boat through a crack in the keel, and to compensate you scoop up the water in a bucket and throw it over the side. As long as you can scoop up the water faster than it comes in through the leak, you can stay afloat and will eventually reach the designated shore. If you stop bailing, however, the boat will sink. Bailing out is only a temporary fix; the real solution is to stop the leak by repairing the crack or re-caulking the keel.

The same thing is true with finances and the economy. A bailout may relieve the pressure for a time, but unless the root cause of the crisis is addressed, the problem will continue. Financial problems are almost never due to insufficient income, but to excessive debt or excessive spending or a combination of both. A "bailout" might help you meet immediate financial obligations, but unless you eliminate your debt and rein in your spending, you will simply need another bailout somewhere down the line. The best solution, in finances as well as in every other area of life, is to build on a solid foundation of time-tested, universally relevant principles. Financial disarray is usually an indicator of disarray in other areas of life such as relationships, personal habits and discipline, and spiritual beliefs and practices.

I think it should be obvious by now, particularly in light of the current state of our nation and economy, that we cannot rely on the government or on "the system" to protect us, provide for us, or help us get ahead. The good news is that we don't need to. God already has a plan for us. He has both the means and the desire to establish us to prosper in every way, not just financially, regardless of the state of the economy.

FACING SOME REALITIES

But before we get more into that, there are several realities that we must consider briefly. First, we need to be reminded that sin always leads to judgment. Someone might ask, "But, Dr. Smith, what does that have to do with the economy, prosperity, and being poor no more?" There are many in the community of faith in our country who are suggesting that the worsening economic conditions we are experiencing may be part of a temporal judgment that God is bringing on our land because of our sins. The Old Testament establishes a clear precedent for God judging nations for the sins of the people, and our nation certainly reflects in many ways the moral and spiritual decadence of those ancient nations, particularly the nation of Israel.

Chapter 28 of Deuteronomy lists the blessings the Israelites could expect from God if they were faithful to obey Him and follow His law. It then goes on to list the curses that would follow if they disobeyed. For instance, if the people were faithful to obey the Lord,

And the Lord will grant you plenty of goods, in the fruit of your body, in the increase of your livestock, and in the produce of your ground, in the land of which the Lord swore to your fathers to give you. The Lord will open to you His good treasure, the heavens, to give the rain to your land in its season, and to bless all the work of your hand. You shall lend to many nations, but you shall not borrow. And the Lord will make you the head and not the tail; you shall be above only, and not be beneath, if you heed the commandments of the Lord your God, which I command you today, and are careful to observe them (Deuteronomy 28:11-13).

If they disobeyed, on the other hand,

Cursed shall be the fruit of your body and the produce of your land, the increase of your cattle and the offspring of your flocks....And your heavens which are over your head shall be bronze, and the earth which is under you shall be iron. The Lord will change the rain of your land to powder and dust; from the heaven it shall come down on you until you are destroyed....The alien who is among you shall rise higher and higher above you, and you shall come down lower and lower. He shall

lend to you, but you shall not lend to him; he shall
be the head, and you shall be the tail (Deuteronomy
28:18,23-24,43-44).

The United States used to be the economic powerhouse of
the world; now we have become a debtor nation, particularly
to China. Our mountainous debt and runaway spending
are fast bringing us as a nation to the point of bankruptcy
and economic disaster. I'm not saying this to be a "gloom
and doom" prophet, but to point out again the fact that we
cannot depend on the government or any of its programs and
entitlements for our prosperity and financial security. Unless
we get our national financial house in order, the day will
soon come when there will *be* no government entitlements
because the government will be out of money. Galatians 1:4
says that Jesus Christ *"gave Himself for our sins, that He might*
deliver us from this present evil age...." Sin brings judgment,
while righteousness brings blessing. We need to be walking
with God in obedience and faith, regardless of what the rest
of the country does, so He will *"deliver us from this present*
evil age," including its negative economic and financial
consequences.

Another reality we must recognize is that most people are
one paycheck away from being homeless. One of the most
fundamental concepts of financial health and prosperity
is to establish the habit of setting aside a portion of each
paycheck into savings in order to build up a reserve. Studies
indicate, however, that the vast majority of Americans, and
particularly the lower and middle classes, have little or no

savings. This means they have no reserve, no backup. All it takes is one serious injury or illness resulting in lost income on the part of the primary breadwinner, and a family faces immediate financial disaster. Our consumer-driven economy does not help the overall dismal savings environment since it constantly encourages consumers to spend money to "stimulate" the economy or offers them easy credit so they can acquire things they neither need nor can afford by enticing them to "buy now and pay later." And they *do* pay later, in a *big* way, paying exorbitant interest rates and spending years trying to dig themselves out of the debt trap.

> YOUR ATTITUDE AND APPROACH TO MONEY WILL AFFECT YOUR RELATIONSHIPS, YOUR WORK, YOUR FAMILY, YOUR FUTURE— EVERYTHING.

Related to this is a third reality, that during times of recession, the rich thrive and the poor become more oppressed. Even during poor economic times, the rich get richer and the poor get poorer. Why is this so? One reason is that the rich have learned the secret of making their money work for them rather than spending all their time working for their money. Most people who struggle financially, including the poor, have never learned the basic principles of sound money management or of how to make their money work for them. Instead, they are thoroughly caught up in our consumer-driven, credit-focused economy that encourages spending and instant gratification. That is a recipe for repeated failure and ongoing financial bondage.

There are implications here that go far beyond the simple subject of finances alone. I said earlier that financial disarray is often an indicator of disarray in other areas of life; in fact, it is often the cause, or catalyst, of disarray in those other areas. For example, financial trouble is one of the top contributing factors behind most troubled marriages. Financial difficulties can sour a marriage faster than anything else, with the possible exception of infidelity. Money problems have broken up marriages and families, destroyed friendships, brought down business partnerships, and shattered the dreams of countless millions. So don't take the subject of money lightly, or assume that it affects only one small area of your life. *Your attitude and approach to money will affect your relationships, your work, your family, your future—everything.* In the New Testament we find that Jesus talked about money more often than any other subject. If He thought it was that important, we should too.

In the light of these three realities, we need to consider a fourth: when you commit yourself and everything you have to God's plan for your life, your economic dilemmas and other issues will be solved. It may not happen overnight, but if you trust in the Lord with all your heart, do not lean on your own understanding, and acknowledge Him in all your ways, He will *"make your paths straight"* (Prov. 3:5-6 NIV). Whatever your current circumstances or condition, God has the ultimate bailout plan for you.

WHAT'S IN YOUR HAND?

The central motif of God's plan is found in the Book of Deuteronomy, where Moses warns the Israelites not to take undue credit for their prosperity and success:

> *You may say to yourself, "My power and the strength of my hands have produced this wealth for me." But remember the Lord your God, for it is he who gives you the ability to produce wealth, and so confirms his covenant, which he swore to your forefathers, as it is today* (Deuteronomy 8:17-18 NIV).

Anything in life that is worth having requires hard work. In finances, as in character, integrity, and life as a whole, there are no shortcuts to wealth and prosperity; no get-rich-quick schemes that will instantly set you up for life. However, you have gifts, talents, and abilities that you can put to work for you to bring you success. Just make sure you remember where they came from. Verse 18 says that it is God who gives us the ability to produce wealth. So I want to ask you, "What's in your hand? What has God placed in your hand that will enable you to acquire and create wealth?" There is something inside you that is unique to you, something that God has given you that makes you different from any other individual. It may be an idea for a product, or a service, or an invention that would benefit other people but that no one is offering. Perhaps you are the one to do so. Maybe you are gifted with mechanical ability, or musical or artistic skill. You may have a book inside of you burning to be written, or a dream of starting your own business. Whatever it is, God has given you something that will bring streams of income to you and move you from where you are to where God wants you to be. What you have to do is discover it and develop it. So I ask you again, "What's in your hand?"

One of the biggest battles most of us have to fight on the way to success in life is the mental battle between what God has planted in our hearts and what society all around us tells us we can or cannot do. Maybe you dream of owning your own business, but your family has always been poor or on the government dole, with several generations of family members limited to unskilled labor and minimum-wage jobs, and no one seems to expect anything more than that out of you. Who are you going to listen to, people of limited vision caught in a rut of mediocrity, or to God and the dream He has placed inside you? Again I ask you, "What's in your hand?"

Someone might object, "But, Dr. Smith, isn't it risky in these uncertain economic times to strike out on a new venture? Wouldn't it be better to play it safe until the economy improves and stabilizes?" Success rarely comes without risk. Show me a successful person and I will show you a risk-taker. I'm not talking about being impulsive; leaping before you look is never wise. But successful risk-takers know when to hold their ground and when to step out. They know when to "play it safe" and when to make their move. It is usually the risk-takers who become the movers and shakers of the world. Most people are not like that. Most people "play it safe" for so long that it becomes a way of life and they never do anything else. The dream that God planted in their hearts slowly fades away until it is all but forgotten; their potential for greatness and for a unique contribution to human society is squandered because they postponed pursuing their dream until a "better time" that never seemed to come.

> THERE IS ALWAYS A PLACE GOD MAKES EXCLUSIVE FROM THE ILLS AND THE INJUSTICES OF: ECONOMIC, POLITICAL, AND SOCIAL UPHEAVAL.

Don't let the fear of risk rob you of becoming everything God wants you to be and receiving all He wants you to receive. Besides, the magnitude of any risk depends on your perspective. The world does not see things the way God sees them. If you are trying to walk with the Lord and follow the dream or passion He has planted in your heart, that which the world might call "risky" is actually the safest and most secure place you could be: in the center of God's will. God is not affected

by the ups and downs and twists and turns of human existence. He is eternal and unchanging, *the same yesterday,
today, and forever"* (Heb. 13:8). The Kingdom of Heaven
is never touched by recession, depression, or economic
uncertainty. Disease, famine, and want are unknown there.
So when you step out in faith to do what God has put
it in your heart to do, you are safe under His care and
protection. It does not matter what is happening in the
world. *Regardless of famine or recession, there is always a
place God makes exclusive from the ills and the injustices of:
economic, political, and social upheaval.*

When you trust in the Lord—when you delight yourself
in Him and commit your ways to Him and look to Him as
your provider and sustainer—you have a place of rest and a
source of inner peace and contentment that empowers you to
ride out every storm of life that comes along. It is a peace that
the secular world knows nothing about, a peace that is beyond
human comprehension. As the apostle Paul advises us:

> *Be anxious for nothing, but in everything by prayer
> and supplication, with thanksgiving, let your requests
> be made known to God; and the peace of God, which
> surpasses all understanding, will guard your hearts and
> minds through Christ Jesus* (Philippians 4:6-7).

The secular world is anxious about many things, but the
children of God are to be anxious about nothing. When we
trust in the Lord, when we bring all our requests to Him,
including all our anxieties and fears, He gives us a peace that

cannot be shaken no matter how much upheaval there is in the world. So even when the economy seems as unstable as the deck of a storm-tossed ship at sea, if you have committed your way to the Lord, you can proceed with confidence.

Many Christians are uncomfortable talking about wealth and prosperity because they are under the impression that it is wrong or sinful to be rich or to desire or pursue material prosperity. They accept as normal reality that some people are going to be rich and some people are going to be poor, with the majority of people falling somewhere in between. As support for their views, they often will cite Scriptures such as the one where Jesus says, *"For you have the poor with you always"* (Mark 14:7a), and the many verses about the poor and about how the people of God are to take care of them. Then there are the warnings and harsh statements about wealth and the wealthy: *"For the love of money is a root of all kinds of evil"* (1 Tim. 6:10a); *"It is easier for a camel to go through the eye of a needle than for a rich man to enter the kingdom of God"* (Mark 10:25).

Although the Bible certainly does contain many such warnings about the seduction and potential dangers of wealth and present severe words for some wealthy people, that is only part of the story. God does not have a problem with your prospering. He does not have a problem with you being rich. Many of the great people of God in the Bible were wealthy: Abraham, Job, Solomon, Nicodemus, Joseph of Arimathea. The Gospels even mention several women who supported Jesus out of their private resources. God has no problem with wealth—in its proper place. Judgment and criticism of the wealthy in the Bible are directed at the greedy, those who have enriched themselves on the backs of the poor or through deceit, graft, bribery, corruption, or other dishonest means. Such people make money their god, and as Jesus said, *"No one can serve two masters....You cannot serve both God and Money"* (Matt. 6:24 NIV). So what is the proper balance? Love God, not money. Serve God, and use money in your service.

Don't Misappropriate Your Gift

With this in mind, as you consider what God has placed in your hand and how you might use it to prosper and become successful, it is very important to be extremely careful that you *don't misappropriate what God has given you.* There are two ways to misappropriate: misuse and neglect. You can misuse what God has given you by squandering it all on yourself, as the prodigal son did, or by wasting it on the wrong things. Just as serious in God's eyes is to neglect what's in your hand, as the unfaithful servant did in Jesus' parable recorded in Matthew 25:14-30. A wealthy man going on a journey entrusted three of his servants with money to use while he was gone. To one servant he gave five talents, to another, two talents, and to the third, one talent. The first two servants quickly went out and through wise investing doubled their money. The third servant, however, was afraid to do anything with his money, so he buried it in the ground for safekeeping until his master returned. When the master returned, he praised and promoted the first two servants, who had used their talents wisely, but the third servant received only condemnation.

There is a certain responsibility that God expects you to have when He places things in your hands. You cannot allow things to control you; you control things. Master your money or it will master you. For example, if you are fortunate to be blessed with an endowment from a grandmother who has passed away, or a sick uncle who has left you with a substantial amount of money, you are responsible before God for how you appropriate those blessings. Give honor to God and acknowledge His Lordship by rendering to Him your tithes and offerings. Establish yourself, not by buying things but by investing wisely in proper vehicles that will increase your income and help you build wealth. Assess the knowledge, skills, abilities, talents, or ideas that you have—that which is in your hand—to see how best to use your available resources to put your gifts to use. Be faithful with what God has placed in your hand and He will bless you. Don't misappropriate what God has given you.

Faithfulness with what God has placed in your hand means showing yourself trustworthy in three specific areas:

> MASTER YOUR MONEY OR IT WILL MASTER YOU.

fiscal accountability, fiscal responsibility, and *fiscal integrity.* The three servants in Jesus' parable were *accountable* to their master for their use of the talents he distributed to them. They knew that when he returned he would call each of them to account for their work. Knowing his master to be a "hard man," the third servant was afraid to touch the talent he had been given for fear of losing it in the wheeling and dealing of the business world, so he did nothing with it except bury it. His inaction brought greater condemnation from his master than if he had tried something—anything—to put his talent to use. In like manner, we are accountable to God for how we use that which He places in our hands.

The third servant demonstrated by his negligence that he was not *responsible* enough to handle the resource he had been given. By contrast, the other two servants showed their worthiness by their skilled and profitable appropriation of their talents. Because they proved themselves responsible with a little, their master entrusted them with much more. Likewise, if we wish to exercise control over the bigger things, we first must prove ourselves responsible with the little things.

Finally, the third servant revealed his lack of *integrity* by blaming his master for his own lack of initiative. According to him, he failed to act because his master was a hard man, but in reality he lacked the character and vision to make the most of the opportunity that he was given. The other two servants, however, demonstrated their integrity not only by the careful and diligent manner in which they handled their master's money, but also by their willingness to give him a full and open account of their actions. Unlike the third servant, they readily "owned up" to their behavior. They had positive returns to show for their work, and their highly pleased master rewarded them. In the same way, if we hope or expect God to bless us when we put to use that which He has placed in our hand, we must be people of integrity, absolutely forthright, upright, transparent, and honest in all our dealings with both God and people.

Currently, our nation is undergoing the most difficult economic circumstances of the past 80 years. Millions of Americans are out of work, many have lost their homes, and the general mood of the people nationwide is a mixture of fear, despair, and anger. There is no doubt about it: many people suffer during times of economic recession or depression. At the same time, there are many others who thrive or continue to do well despite the overall negative state of the economy. While many people lose money and lose ground financially, there are others who continue to gain ground, who continue to make money, who continue to move into greater and greater wealth. For them, it doesn't matter what the government says, or what the economists say, or the news media, or the financial prognosticators, or the politicians, or the Wall Street gurus. Even during times of economic downturn and general financial hardship, there are those who defy all expectations and prosper regardless.

What makes the difference? Why do some prosper and do well, even during difficult times, while others struggle to stay afloat? There is more to it than chance or luck. Success is almost never accidental. Those who succeed, even in the midst of economic difficulties, do so because they have three things going for them: *knowledge, positioning,* and *preparation.* They have *knowledge* of money and markets and how they work; they have *positioned* themselves for success by walking in humble submission to God and by applying time-tested principles of prosperity; and they have *prepared* themselves for success by understanding their gifts, talents, and abilities, and by identifying what God has placed in their hand.

If you want to succeed in finances as well as in all of life, you have to begin where you are. So I ask you again, *"What's in your hand?"*

Chapter Three

TEN RULES OF PROSPERITY

Prosperity, I think it is safe to say, is on everybody's mind these days, particularly in our current economic climate. The economic recession that began in 2008 has given way to a flat, anemic "recovery" characterized by stubbornly and unacceptably high unemployment, a volatile stock market, and a general sense of uncertainty, discouragement, and fear. Americans have seen the value of their homes shrink along with their dollar while gasoline prices have doubled over the past two years. Prices have increased for almost everything while many Americans have experienced a loss in buying power due to the dropping value of the dollar. The question everyone seems to be asking is, "What lies ahead for us and our nation: prosperity or austerity?"

The answer to that question depends on many factors, not the least of which is the application of time-tested principles of prosperity that work even in austere times. Before we examine these principles, however, it is important to note exactly what we mean by the word *prosperity* because it has to do with a lot more than just money.

Prosperity is defined as "the condition of being successful or thriving," especially in the sense of "economic well-being." And although we tend to think of prosperity most often in economic terms, this is only one aspect of the word's meaning. In addition to financial stability, prosperity can apply to our health and welfare as well as to our personal, family, and social relationships; indeed, every area of life. A happy family characterized by mutual love, affirmation, and support, for example, is a prosperous family even if they don't have a great deal of money. And all of us, I am sure, can think of families we have heard of that are financially well-off yet torn by internal strife, resentment, competition, bitterness, and bad blood. Can such a family truly be called prosperous? After all, prosperity ultimately has to do with happiness, and no amount of money can buy happiness. Neither can it buy permanent security. This is the point Jesus was making when He asked, *"For what will it profit a man if he gains the whole world, and loses his own soul?"* (Mark 8:36).

In a related sense, the verb *prosper* means "to succeed in an enterprise or activity," especially "to achieve economic success." But it also means "to become strong and flourishing" and "to cause to succeed or thrive." Likewise, the adjective *prosperous* describes "auspicious" and "favorable" circumstances; conditions "marked by success or economic well-being; enjoying vigorous and healthy growth."

It should be clear from all these definitions that the condition of prosperity touches a much broader field than economics and finances alone. So when we talk about the ten rules or principles of prosperity, we're talking about more than just money and financial wealth. We want to take the broad picture, as expressed in these words by the apostle John: *"Beloved, I pray that you may prosper **in all things** and be in health, just **as your soul prospers**"* (3 John 2, emphasis added).

Why settle for superficial prosperity in one area (material wealth) when prosperity in the totality of life is within your reach? True wealth is more than money; it is a state of abiding contentment and overall well-being. Are you content with your life? Are you at peace with God, yourself, and others? Can you accept your present circumstances with equanimity even if you have not yet arrived at the place

> FOR CHILDREN OF GOD, PROSPERITY IS A DESTINY.

in life where you want to be? Prosperity *"in all things"* is as much about the journey as it is the destination. Contentment lies in learning to love and affirm and enjoy life *now* even though you have not yet reached all your goals or realized all your dreams. This kind of life contentment is something that the world outside of Christ knows nothing about. In the world, prosperity involves cutthroat competition, dog-eat-dog demeanor, and shrewd scheming. For children of the world, prosperity is a goal; for children of God, it is a *destiny*. This being so, as children of God we can be content along the way, knowing that our circumstances at any given time are only steps in the process of arriving at the "future" and the "hope" that God has planned for us (see Jer. 29:11). The apostle Paul described the difference this way:

> *Now godliness with contentment is great gain. For we brought nothing into this world, and it is certain we can carry nothing out. And having food and clothing, with these we shall be content. But those who desire to be rich fall into temptation and a snare, and into many foolish and harmful lusts which drown men in destruction and perdition. For the love of money is a root of all kinds of evil, for which some have strayed from the faith in their greediness, and pierced themselves through with many sorrows. But you, O man of God, flee these things and pursue righteousness, godliness, faith, love, patience, gentleness. Fight the good fight of faith, lay hold on eternal life, to which you were also called and have confessed the good confession in the presence of many witnesses* (1 Timothy 6:6-12).

There are several important points to note here. The first is that contentment and godliness go together. Without godliness there can be no true contentment. As Saint Augustine wrote of God in his *Confessions* at the end of the fourth century, "Thou madest us for Thyself, and our heart is restless, until it repose in Thee." We would never be content—or truly prosperous—until our hearts rest in the Lord.

Second, since we bring nothing material into this world and take nothing out of it, we need to hold with a light touch those material things that come to us during this life. We must not become obsessed with clutching tightly anything that we cannot take with us when we die. Besides, those things do not belong to us anyway; they belong to God, who created all things. By virtue of His love and grace, He allows us to use material things for the pleasure and benefit of ourselves and others.

Third, the love of God leads to joy and life, while love of money leads to sorrow and destruction. Consider those things that Paul associates with the love of money: temptation, snare, foolish and harmful lusts, destruction, perdition, evil, greediness, and sorrows. In contrast, look at the characteristics of the *"man of God,"* which includes *all* who love Him: righteousness, godliness, faith, love, patience, gentleness, and, most of all, eternal life. Here we have a description of *true prosperity*. This is what it means to say that we *"prosper in all things…as* [our] *soul prospers."*

With these considerations in mind, let's look now at ten time-tested and trustworthy rules or principles of prosperity. But be warned: If you are looking for an easy path or a quick fix for your problems, you won't find it here. These rules will work, like all sound principles, but they do not operate automatically or in the abstract. If you want them to work for you, you will have to apply them consciously and deliberately, and this will require time and effort on your part. The greatest struggle you will face is the struggle between your disciplined mind and your undisciplined mind. *Mental discipline is the key to success,* so stay alert. Nothing in life worth accomplishing comes without focus and attention.

PROSPERITY RULE #1: NEVER START DRIVING WITHOUT KNOWING WHERE YOU ARE GOING.

If you were to set out on a road trip to a place you have never been before, with no idea how to get there, and with no road maps or GPS to guide you, before long you would find yourself completely lost. As with travel, a safe and sound arrival at your destination in life can be assured only through careful advance planning. Knowing where you want to go is one thing; planning the route to get you there is another. One place to start is by identifying a vision. Just as the windshield of your car helps you see the road ahead, a vision of where you want to go helps you chart the course of your life. Ask yourself some questions. What is most important to you in life? Where do you want to go? Where do you want to be five years from now in your career or profession? In your income level? Where do you want to be living five years from now? What are your dreams for your family? Do you know your spouse's dreams? Your children's? What place will faith in Christ and the church have in your life and in the life of your family?

Once you have identified your destination, the next step is to chart out the path that will get you there. What resources, assets, skills, abilities, and knowledge do you already have that will help you move toward fulfilling your vision? Which of those things will you need to acquire, and how will you do it? Will you need to go back to school?

These are just a few of the questions you may want to ask yourself as you set your sights on preparing yourself for a prosperous future. One thing is certain: On your journey through life you will encounter both pain and pleasure. These are the two main signposts on the highway toward your dreams, and both have important roles to play. None of us like pain, but it is an inevitable part of life. But if we have the right mind-set, we can learn from our pain. Mistakes can be painful, even costly, but we can learn from them what not to do and be wiser for it. We tend to grow the most through painful circumstances, so don't fear the pain of life. Don't go looking for pain, but when it comes, acknowledge its presence and ask the Lord to help you learn from the experience. Pleasure, on the other hand, is one of the "perks" of life that refresh us and encourage us to continue the journey.

One final point to consider when planning your journey: You will never reach the apex in life as long as you confine yourself to the ordinary and normal. If you are going to reach the zenith, you are going to have to be willing to climb out of the box, engage in some innovative possibility thinking, and do something extraordinary.

PROSPERITY RULE #2: THE EMPTY SPACE IN FRONT OF YOU IS PREGNANT WITH NEVER-ENDING POTENTIAL AND POSSIBILITY.

No matter who you are, you were born with never-ending potential and possibility. Regardless of your age, whether you are young, middle-aged, or a senior citizen, you have barely scratched the surface of what you are capable of doing and creating. Your past experiences or current circumstances do not matter; God has given you unbelievable and outrageous abilities in every area of your life. Learn to think creatively about the things and the situations around you. Don't limit yourself to only what you can see in any given situation. Stop seeing things only as they are and start imagining them as they could be. That promotion at work that you want but have always assumed that you will never get... Why not? That idea you have for an invention or for an innovative business solution but don't know where to start and feel it will probably never "fly" anyway... Why not? Don't focus on all the reasons why it will never work; start thinking about all the reasons it will. That dilapidated old shed in your backyard that you think is useless and should probably be torn down... Why? What if it could be repaired? What if it could be turned into a workshop in which you create a masterpiece? Recognizing potential is a matter of looking beyond what is to what can be. It is a matter of learning to look through different eyes: the eyes of your imagination. God has placed virtually unlimited potential in you, and the apparently barren circumstances around you are actually pregnant God-given possibilities. Look for them. Bring your potential to bear in bringing life to the possibilities all around you.

PROSPERITY RULE #3: CHANGE YOUR THINKING.

The average person suffers from a condition we could call "stinking thinking." Stinking thinking is a mind-set that dwells on negativity; it always likes to point out all the reasons why something cannot be done or why circumstances cannot change. The tragedy of stinking thinking is that so often it is based on misunderstanding and even outright error. Do you assume you will never get ahead because someone once told you that you would never amount to anything? If so, you are a victim of stinking thinking. It's time to change your thinking. The Bible says, *"As* [a man] *thinks in his heart, so is he"* (Prov. 23:7a).

All of us are the product of our thoughts. Our thought processes determine the way we live our lives. Simple observation can tell you a lot about people and the mind-set that drives their lives: the way they walk, talk, eat, and dress; even their posture and mannerisms. Whatever seeds have been sown and cultivated in a person's mind will determine whether that person has a mind-set of poverty and lack or abundance and prosperity; of pessimism or optimism; of low expectations or high hopes; of limited options or unlimited opportunities.

Most people have been programmed to live a life of average. Mother, father, friends, relatives, or others suggest that they subscribe to a life of mediocrity. Rarely is this explicit; more often it is implicit, implied by words, attitudes, and behaviors that fortify a mundane life of low expectations and underachievement.

Maybe that is your story. Has there ever been a time in your life when you were persuaded to reach beyond the gates of average? When a quiet inner voice said, "I can rise higher," or "I can do more," or "I can be better"? The apostle Paul links the quality of our thinking to our ability to know and do the will of God: *"And do not be conformed to this world, but be transformed by the renewing of your mind, that you may prove what is that good and acceptable and perfect will of God"* (Rom. 12:2). To be *"conformed to this world"* means, in part, to go along with the stinking thinking that characterizes the mind-set of most people. Renewing your mind, on the other hand, involves learning to think creatively, like the Creator who gave you your mind; to build the habit of possibility thinking and reject the negative mind-set that is always telling you why you can't do something.

So my question to you is, "What are you thinking?" What's on your mind right now? Maybe you lost your job, are having trouble finding another one, and wonder how you're going to take care of your family. Perhaps you have a job but are dissatisfied because you feel it has no future and is not really what you want to be doing anyway. Restlessness about your work or a time of forced transition such as a job loss may be God's indicator to you that it is time to change your situation and move up. No matter who you are, man or woman, you are pregnant with something—a dream, a vision, an idea, a product or service, a book, a business—that is waiting to be born. Whatever it is, God may be saying to you, "The time is now."

In the movie *Up in the Air*, George Clooney plays a human resource specialist who flies all over the country and fires people. During one scene a man who has just been fired asks in bewilderment, "What do I do now?" Looking over the man's résumé, Clooney's character replies, "Sam, you always wanted to be a baker. You were a great chef. I see here that you had tremendous potential."

Could it be that you lost your job or are restless where you are because God wants you to recover a dream that is all but lost and reach into the destiny that He has for you? Have you had jobs handling money? Have you worked in accounts payable or accounts receivable? Perhaps God has been setting you up with the knowledge you need to start and run your own business. Whoever you are and whatever your situation, take inventory of your past experiences to discover that for which God has been preparing you. Be encouraged! Get up! Change your thinking! Your future awaits you!

PROSPERITY RULE #4: WEALTH HAS TO TAKE UP RESIDENCY IN YOU.

Deuteronomy 8:18 says that it is God who gives us the power or ability to acquire wealth. What does this mean? It means that God has placed inside each one of us a creative genius, a wealth - creating giant lying dormant until stirred to life. Let's call it "You, Inc." Everything you need to take the leap into prosperity already resides in you. Your challenge is to find and develop the talents and skills with which God has gifted you. This requires faith. First, you must believe God; you must believe Him when He says He has given you the ability to acquire wealth. He wants you to succeed, and if you trust Him, He will help you along the way. Second, you must believe in yourself; you must throw out all the negatives that people have spoken into your life in the past. In the end, the only opinion that matters is God's opinion, and He believes in you. So believe in yourself. Don't be afraid to invest in your dreams and your future. Any dream worth having is worth taking the time to prepare. Even if your dream is to build a business that will make a profit and create jobs for others, you must first invest in yourself. "You, Inc." is the corporation of your life. Invest heavily in it. Get more education, if that is what you need. Develop yourself. Construct a "business plan" to take you from your present to your future. Invest in yourself so that as you grow you can invest in others.

PROSPERITY RULE #5: STAY FOCUSED.

Many people quit before their dreams come to fruition because they have focus issues. If you are like most people, you don't have a money problem or a skill problem; you have a focus problem. Most of the time, incompleteness in our lives can be traced back, at least in part, to a lack of focus. The good news is that it is never too late to become more focused. By focus, I mean identifying the activities that are most critical to the advancement of your dream and zeroing in on them while relegating noncritical activities to the background. There are many good things in which you could invest your time that are enjoyable and even profitable, but not all of them will move you toward your dream. Learning to focus will help you avoid the trap of confusing busyness with progress. Don't waste time being busy for the sake of being busy. Most people are busy but not effective because they have never learned to focus. Focus on your strengths, the things that excite you, and the truly important concerns of life—God, family, and church—and you will *prosper in all things...as your soul prospers.*

PROSPERITY RULE #6: LOSE THE LOSERS.

Prosperity comes to those who are prepared for it. Most people are not prepared for prosperity, either mentally or situationally. That may sound surprising, but it is verified out of experience. When asked, most people will say that they would like to be prosperous, but few possess the knowledge or the will to do what is necessary to achieve it. By situational preparedness I mean deliberately positioning oneself for prosperity. Positioning yourself for prosperity involves many things, but one of the most important is to place yourself in the proximity of winners. This means that you must lose the losers. I call it "LTL."

Lose the losers. Disconnect from your negative past. Your past tells lies about your future. If you want to position yourself for prosperity, one of the things you have to do is choose your friends carefully. Just because you are friends with someone does not necessarily mean that that person will help you move ahead. As you set your heart and mind to advance toward your destiny, you need to understand that not everyone you know is with you. Some people, by their language, attitude, and lifestyle, will only drag you down. Lose them. Real friends are like a spotter with weights; they will push you forward to your destiny. Those are the people you want to hang with. Please understand me: I am not saying that you should coldly and heartlessly dump longtime friends or acquaintances just because they don't share your vision of the future. What I am saying is that you need to carefully and thoughtfully re-examine your relationships to identify those people who can help you achieve your goals and those who cannot. Then you must resolve to spend more time with the former and less with the latter. You have to have the right people speaking into your life, so choose them carefully. Enjoy all your friends at whatever level of friendship you have with them, but latch onto those whose wisdom you respect and whose investment in your life can help you move forward.

This principle of losing the losers is also sound biblical counsel. We all have the tendency to become like the people we spend time with, and the Bible tells us that if we want to succeed, if we want to prosper and be blessed, we must avoid associating with the wrong kind of people:

Blessed is the man who walks not in the counsel of the ungodly, nor stands in the path of sinners, nor sits in the seat of the scornful; but his delight is in the law of the Lord, and in His law he meditates day and night. He shall be like a tree planted by the rivers of water, that brings forth its fruit in its season, whose leaf also shall not wither; and whatever he does shall prosper (Psalm 1:1-3).

Don't let your past determine your future. You are not a failure. No matter how many times you have failed in the past, no matter how many times you have dropped the ball, no matter how many times you have fallen, you are not a failure as long as you keep getting up and learn from your mistakes. The only time you fail is when you give up or continue to make the same mistake over and over. Letting your past determine your future is thinking in reverse. It is like trying to drive a car by using only the rearview mirror and never looking out the windshield. You will never enter your future destiny by looking backward all the time. Don't try to back into your future. Disconnect from your negative past. Lose the losers. Look ahead, and keep pressing forward.

PROSPERITY RULE #7: YOU WILL NEVER GET TO THE PALACE TALKING LIKE A PEASANT.

If you want to be prosperous, you must think like a prosperous person and you must talk like a prosperous person. This is not just empty posturing. We have already discussed the importance of changing your thinking; now you must change your speech to match. Thoughts give birth to speech, and our speech has a funny way of influencing the course of our lives. If you want to be a winner, think and talk like a winner. No more "trash talk." No more putting yourself down. No more negativity.

Prosperous people don't waste time knowing what they want one minute and then sinking back into fear and doubt the next. This only attracts confusion and anxiety. Get the confusion and anxiety out of your life. Anyone or anything that brings you confusion; anyone or anything that brings you drama; anyone or anything that brings you anxiety—cut those people or things out of your life now.

Focus your mind on positive and worthwhile things and let your speech follow suit. In other words, change your speech to match your change in thinking. Take to heart these wise words from the apostle Paul:

Finally, brethren, whatever things are true, whatever things are noble, whatever things are just, whatever things are pure, whatever things are lovely, whatever things are of good report, if there is any virtue and if there is anything praiseworthy—meditate on these things (Philippians 4:8).

If then you were raised with Christ, seek those things which are above, where Christ is, sitting at the right hand of God. Set your mind on things above, not on things on the earth (Colossians 3:1-2).

Let no corrupt word proceed out of your mouth, but what is good for necessary edification, that it may impart grace to the hearers (Ephesians 4:29).

Stop thinking and talking like the person you are and start thinking and talking like the person you want to be. If you don't think like a prosperous person, you won't be; if you don't talk like a prosperous person, you won't be. Take control of your life! Don't allow yourself to be cornered or trapped in situations that you know will be a breeding ground for confusion and anxiety.

PROSPERITY RULE #8: ALWAYS HAVE SEVERAL STREAMS OF INCOME.

Successful people always have more than one thing going on. Financially, they try to open and maintain as many different streams of income as possible: salary, stocks and bonds, real estate, rental income, oil and natural gas royalties, royalties from books or other published writings, other types of investments; you name it. Referring to life in general, this prosperity rule means keeping all your options open and always being on the lookout for opportunities to expand your wealth, build new relationships, and improve your life and the lives of those you love. If you want to prosper, take off the blinders; get rid of your tunnel vision. Liberate yourself from narrow-minded thinking and assumptions that only limit you. By maximizing your options and positioning yourself for any opportunity that comes along, you can insulate yourself and your family against the negative effects of downturns or setbacks. If one promising income stream or option suddenly closes, you have alternatives without having to scramble frantically to avoid losing ground.

Successful people also understand that the biggest key to true wealth is passive income: income that will continue to flow even if you are no longer able to work, such as rental income, returns on investments, royalties, etc. Examine your situation carefully and identify areas in your life where you can begin to diversify.

PROSPERITY RULE #9: EARN MORE THAN YOU SPEND.

One of the most fundamental principles of financial management is to earn more than you spend. But this principle applies to all areas of life, not just finances. There are many different ways to state this principle. Live within your means. Don't bite off more than you can chew. Don't take on more than you can handle. Don't burn the candle at both ends. Contentment, as we discussed earlier, really comes into play here. Don't let yourself become obsessed with "keeping up with the Joneses." Focus on what is right for you, your family, and your situation, and don't worry about what other people are doing. Always remember that in every area of life, whether finances, time, energy, activity, relationships, or anything else, your revenues must exceed your expenditures; your income must be greater than your outgo. Even Jesus could not give all the time without a break. He needed periodic times of quiet and solitude to refresh Himself. It is the same with you and me. If your revenues do not exceed your expenditures, you are on a course for destruction and failure.

Prosperity Rule #10: Money is not your enemy; money is your friend.

Finally, drill into your head the principle that money is your friend, not your enemy. The difference lies in how you understand money. Is money your dream, or is money merely one tool among many that helps you achieve your dream? If money is your dream, money will master you and you will be its slave. Realizing that money is merely a tool to be used, however, will allow you to master money and make it work for you. Most people are slaves to money and don't even know it. Money and the desire for more rule their lives and consume their waking thoughts. When money is your master, it affects every area of your life in a negative way. A slave has no rights and no life to call his own, but lives only to do the will of his master. Don't be a slave to money. Instead, master your money and make it your friend, and this will help position you for a life of true prosperity.

Chapter Four

It's Time to Get Up

Have you ever woke up in the morning, glanced at the clock through bleary, sleep-filled eyes, and immediately wanted to just pull the covers over your head and go back to sleep? Sometimes you can, depending upon the day or the occasion, but most of the time you can't. You have to get up because you have a job, and if you don't show up you will be fired. You have to get up because you are in school and if you do not go to class you will flunk out. You have to get up because your spouse and your children are depending on you. You have to get up because you have obligations to meet and promises to keep. You have to get up because you can't get things done or get ahead in life by staying in bed all the time.

I once saw someone wearing a T-shirt with these words on the front: "I'm up and dressed. What more do you want?" Although this sentiment humorously captures the way we all feel sometimes, it also expresses an important truth: *getting up is a fundamental principle of life.*

Getting up is basic to prosperity and success in every arena or endeavor of life. It has been said that successful people are not people who have never been knocked down, but people who keep getting up until finally they get up one time more often than they are knocked down. There will always be circumstances in life that will knock you down— loss of a job, death in the family, financial setback, debilitating injury or illness, loss of a home from fire or a natural disaster, etc. What you have to decide when life knocks you down is whether you will stay down for the count or get up and keep fighting. Many people never realize their dreams because they give up too soon. They get knocked down so many times that they grow weary of the struggle. Discouragement overwhelms them to the point where they simply give up. Who knows but that success might have come had they just gotten up

> GETTING UP CAN BE THE DECIDING FACTOR BETWEEN SUCCESS AND FAILURE.

one more time? No matter how discouraged you are, no matter how difficult or hopeless your situation may seem, don't surrender to hopelessness. I can promise you this: your success in any area of life is virtually guaranteed as long as you keep getting up.

Getting up can be the deciding factor between success and failure. Success never comes without determination and hard work. Failure is easy, however: simply do nothing. The Bible draws a clear distinction between the rewards of industry and hard work and the consequences of laziness and sloth. Nowhere is this distinction drawn more clearly than in the Book of Proverbs.

> *He who has a slack hand becomes poor, but the hand of the diligent makes rich* (Proverbs 10:4).

A *"slack hand"* (laziness) results in poverty, but diligence (getting up and working) leads to prosperity.

> *The hand of the diligent will rule, but the lazy man will be put to forced labor* (Proverbs 12:24).

People who get up will *"rule"* (be community leaders, people of influence and high reputation, possibly own their own business), while lazy people will never get ahead, never achieve their dreams, and get trapped in a cycle of dead-end jobs.

> *The soul of a lazy man desires, and has nothing; but the soul of the diligent shall be made rich* (Proverbs 13:4).

Lazy people have just as many dreams and desires as others do, but they lack the drive to do the necessary work to make them come true. They would rather have everything they want handed to them. The diligent, on the other hand, will succeed richly because they know that they have to get up and put feet to their dreams.

> *The lazy man will not plow because of winter; he will beg during harvest and have nothing* (Proverbs 20:4).

Because the lazy man will not plow (work) in proper season, he will never have the things he needs.

> *The desire of the lazy man kills him, for his hands refuse to labor* (Proverbs 21:25).

Because a lazy man lacks the drive to pursue his dreams, his dreams die a slow death and his hopes die with them.

> *The plans of the diligent lead surely to plenty, but those of everyone who is hasty, surely to poverty* (Proverbs 21:5).

Diligent people, those who get up, plan carefully for prosperity and are rewarded. Hasty people, those who are too lazy to plan thoroughly and settle for haphazard efforts, will not succeed.

RISE AND SHINE!

Throughout the Bible we find the principle of "getting up" stated or implied in many different ways. One of the most direct is found in the writings of the prophet Isaiah:

Arise, shine; for your light has come! And the glory of the Lord is risen upon you. For behold, the darkness shall cover the earth, and deep darkness the people; but the Lord will arise over you, and His glory will be seen upon you. The Gentiles shall come to your light, and kings to the brightness of your rising (Isaiah 60:1-3).

In these verses the command to "get up" (*"arise"*) is presented in the context of restoration and renewed prosperity for the people of God upon coming out of a period of exile, disgrace, and sorrow. Isaiah was the most highly educated of all the Old Testament prophets, a fact that is evident in the book that bears his name, which biblical scholars uniformly agree is a literary masterpiece. These verses are found toward the end of the book in a section devoted to prophecies and promises of the blessings and favor God's people would enjoy upon their return from Babylonian exile. Since Isaiah lived in the eighth century B.C. and the Babylonian exile of the Jews in the southern kingdom of Judah did not occur until the sixth century B.C., the prophet is referring to events that would take place as much as 200 years after his own day. When those Jewish exiles returned to their homeland after 70 years of captivity, they would find their capital city of Jerusalem in ruins and the great Temple of Solomon, which to them represented the very presence of God in their midst, destroyed. They would be wrestling with the issue of whether or not God would work in their situation and cause them to prosper again. Could their farms and fields thrive again? Could they rise to their former greatness as a nation? Would they ever know the blessings and favor of God again?

Speaking prophetically as much as 200 years in advance, Isaiah speaks hope to the people with the promise that a new day is coming. He assures them that God has not forgotten them and that their mission still is to be a light to the world. God does not change and His purposes never change. He had called the Israelites to be His own special chosen people, and since the call of God is irrevocable, His purpose for them was still in effect regardless of their failures. Isaiah wanted them to take comfort in the promise of a new day.

The passage begins with a command. In verse 1 Isaiah exhorts the people to *"arise."* This one word sets the tone for the entire chapter. The Hebrew word for "arise" in this verse is *qum*, which has a range of meanings including to "stand up," to "get up" as to get out of bed in the morning, to "raise up," to "confirm," and to "establish" something. So with this one word Isaiah is saying to the people, "Get up and take your stand. Be confirmed and established in your abundant future as the people of God." The entire chapter speaks of the blessings, favor, and abundance that will come to God's people in the days ahead, but it begins with the command to *"arise."* They must get up because the day of their prosperity is at hand.

To arise in this sense also means to be confirmed in or established. Stated another way, to arise or to get up means that you have to consciously and deliberately *position* yourself for prosperity. In order to do this, you must "get up" in three specific ways.

First, you must get up *psychologically*. You have to change your thinking; you must develop a new mind-set. We saw this in the previous chapter. Changing your thinking is one of the ten rules of prosperity. Today's thinking will not take you where you want to be tomorrow. You must renew your mind on a daily basis. This does not mean that you are constantly altering your beliefs or values, but that you keep your thinking fresh. It means finding ways to challenge your mind on a regular basis to keep yourself out of a mental rut. It means always looking for innovative solutions to problems and creative ways to meet challenges. It means learning to look at each new day as a new opportunity rather than as a continuation of the same unending drudgery. Depending on your attitude, you can make today better than yesterday and tomorrow better than today.

KEEP YOUR THINKING FRESH.

There is a great deal of power in possibility thinking. In many ways we are what we think. Our self-image and self-expectations tend to become self-fulfilling prophecies. If you do not expect to succeed, you probably won't; if you do not believe that your situation can change, it probably won't. You cannot shoot for the stars—much less reach them—if your sights are set on the ground at your feet. Stop assuming that your dreams are out of reach. Get rid of the self-defeating thought patterns that say, "I'm not good enough," or "I'm not smart enough," or "There are too many things working against me," or "No one in my family has ever amounted to much, and I am no different." You *are* different—or you *can* be! Your past does not have to determine your future. Where you are today does not have to determine where you will be tomorrow. Don't be discouraged because no one believes in you. Believe in yourself. Even more, believe in God, for He believes in you. God wants you to succeed in every dimension of life. He has dreams and plans for you that are bigger than anything you can possibly imagine. God has placed inside you the potential for greatness; don't let it die unborn. The only person who can hold you back is *you*, and your mind-set is the key. There is more at stake here than just your personal progress. Your family, your children, will follow your lead. Your mind-set will become their mind-set. So shake off the mental cobwebs. Rouse yourself from the doldrums of impossibility thinking. Get up psychologically and position yourself mentally for the success that is your destiny—and your descendants' after you.

In addition to getting up psychologically you also have to get up *socially*. Although this is related to Prosperity Rule #6, *Lose the losers*, it also has a wider application. As I discussed in Chapter Three, choosing your friends carefully is vitally important to your success. You must exercise discernment concerning who you allow to speak into your life because not everyone's counsel, advice, or opinion will be good for you.

Getting up socially involves more than the decisions you make about other people, however; it also involves the way you spend your time. How much time do you waste every day in pursuits that will never help you get where you want to go? What do you do when you get home from work? Do you kick back for hours in front of the television, or do you spend your time building relationships with your family and friends? Do you let your mind go on autopilot or do you engage it regularly through reading and study to gain knowledge and broaden the horizon of your skills and abilities?

Examine your options. If you seem locked into a status quo that is taking you nowhere, what resources are available to help you rise above, move ahead, and break out of that status quo? Can you learn a new trade? Go back to school? Are there ways for you to network with people who do what you want to do and who are where you want to be—people whose wisdom, knowledge, and

HOW DO YOU SPEND YOUR TIME?

experience you can tap into? We live in an increasingly high-tech, computerized society that has placed vast amounts of knowledge and information at our fingertips at a level undreamed of only a generation or two ago. Although this affords us great benefits, it also makes it very easy for us to pursue these things in isolation. Today you can read, study, do your banking, pay your bills, watch your favorite movies and television shows, and do all your shopping, including your groceries, online without ever having to set foot outside your door. Human beings are social creatures by design. We thrive best when we live in regular contact with others.

Don't misunderstand me. I'm not saying you should never take a break or spend time alone. Times of solitude and times of leisure both are important for a healthy, balanced life. But with a little planning, even your down times can serve to help you move toward your goals. Instead of watching that rerun you've seen a dozen times before, watch a documentary or read a book, or play a game with your family. It is very easy to slip into habits of activity (or inactivity) that will keep you stuck on dead center. Getting up socially means taking an honest look at where you are and making a deliberate decision to change your lifestyle in ways that will break you free of the bonds of the mental and social habits that are holding you back.

Third, in order to position yourself for prosperity and posterity, you have to get up *physically*. You have to physically get up and do something for yourself. It is important to dream and to plan and to talk about what you want to do and what you want to see come to pass in your life and the lives of those whom you love, but talk alone is cheap. Unless you invest plenty of shoe leather and sweat equity, you will never realize your dreams. The worst kind of person to be around is a person who does a lot of talking but with whom nothing ever transpires; a person who never finishes anything. Most people have big dreams but few see their dreams come true. What makes the difference?

Although many have dreams, few possess the drive, the will, the belief in themselves, and the confidence in their destiny to invest the time and effort necessary to realize their dreams. Successful people, in other words, are those who get up physically and commit themselves to the hard work of converting their dreams into reality.

Too many people today seem to want or expect success and prosperity to be handed to them on a silver platter. Unfortunately, life does not work that way. A welfare mentality never leads to success; it merely keeps people in bondage. Prosperity and success will continue to elude people who insist on staying on the dole. This is why, in order to position yourself for prosperity, you must get up psychologically, socially, and physically. If you want a strong and healthy marriage, for example, you have to work at it. You have to invest time and energy being physically present and available to your spouse, consciously and deliberately building that relationship. If you want to truly succeed in your vocation and build a successful career rather than just hold a job, you have to be willing to invest more of yourself

UNLESS YOU INVEST PLENTY OF SHOE LEATHER AND SWEAT EQUITY, YOU WILL NEVER REALIZE YOUR DREAMS.

than the bare minimum required by your employer. Be enthusiastic. Become an idea person, one who sets the pace rather than follows the trend. Don't simply fill a space and work for a paycheck; invest yourself in your job by looking to the future. Dress, talk, think, and behave according to where you want to be in the future, not to where you are now.

Another aspect of getting up physically that is too important to ignore involves nutrition and exercise. Don't underestimate the effect that a balanced diet and regular physical activity (or the lack of them) will have on your mental alertness and bodily stamina. Cut the junk food. Go for real nutrition: fresh fruits, vegetables, grains, lean meats, etc. in balanced portions. Try to adjust your schedule so you can avoid eating on the run. Join a health club or at least try to get in one or two good brisk walks every day. Even small changes in your routine now can bring big benefits later.

It's one thing to talk about the importance of getting up, but quite another to actually do it. Failure to get up is the root cause behind many other failures in life: failure in school, failure at work, failure at home, failure in marriage, failure in interpersonal relationships, failure to realize one's dreams, failure with finances, and failure to plan for the future. Why do so many people fail in life, or at least settle for a mundane, humdrum existence? Because they fail to get up. Getting up always involves change, and change makes a lot of people uncomfortable.

Enemies to Prosperity

There are two enemies that we all must confront and overcome in order to prosper—enemies that will keep us from getting up unless we fight them off. The first enemy is *fear*. One of the things that many people fear the most is change. Generally speaking, the older we get the more we become creatures of routine. Routine is comfortable, familiar, and nonthreatening. Change disrupts routine; it yanks us out our comfort zone, leaving us feeling disoriented, naked, and vulnerable. It seems so much easier simply to stay where we are, nestled in the cozy little niche we have carved out for ourselves. Getting up always means changing our position, and many of us would rather not be bothered. The thought of change scares us too much. Our minds swirl with all sorts of questions. "What if I fail? What if I risk change and lose what I have? What will other people think if I do this? What will my family say? What will my friends say?" Some people fear failure so much that they never attempt anything, and therefore fail at life. Fear is a crippler that hamstrings us, causing us to quit the game and hobble to the bench, sidelined for the rest of the season, or even for life.

The second great enemy of getting up is *fatigue*. Often we fail to get up because we are simply too tired. The ups and downs of life have worn us out. It is too much work simply to think, much less to get up and actually do something. Life in this world is full of uncertainties and unknowns, and the constant battle to make our way in the world and keep ourselves and our loved ones afloat often leaves us in a state of mental, emotional, and physical fatigue. We are convinced that we do not have the strength or the energy to take another step.

Fear and fatigue are related; they feed on each other. Fear saps our strength and our confidence, so that we feel tired and weary. And when we are tired, our minds magnify our fears. This quickly becomes a vicious cycle that, once ingrained, is very difficult to break. I wish I had a secret formula or a three-step plan to give you for beating the enemies of fear and fatigue, but I don't because there are none. What you have to do is decide within yourself that you are not going to give in to these enemies any longer but are going to get up in spite of your fatigue and change your position in spite of your fear. Once you do this, you will discover that fear and fatigue are like schoolyard bullies: Stand up to them and they will back down; refuse to be intimidated and they will be knocked down to size.

I like to work out at the gym and do so often. Any athlete or anyone else who works out regularly will tell you that the hardest battle you will fight is the battle to get yourself to the gym. Your mind will assail you with all sorts of reasons or excuses why you shouldn't go today, or why you need to put this off until tomorrow. The only way your workout plan will work is for you to *work*! There is no substitute. You will not overcome fear or fatigue by osmosis, or by lying in your bed hoping for the best. No matter the fear that maybe nibbling at your heart, or the fatigue that makes your body or mind feel like it weighs a ton, you've got to sit up, plant your feet on the floor, and *get up* and get moving! This is true not only for getting to the gym, but also for getting through life. If you want a strong body, you have to work at it. If you want a strong marriage, you have to work at it. If you want a strong financial condition, you have to work at it. If you want to be strong in your job, vocation, or chosen profession, you have to work at it. And the first step in going to work is to get up.

Where do we find the resources to defeat the enemies of fear and fatigue? Once again, we can turn to the Book of Isaiah, which contains these powerful promises:

Fear not, for I am with you; be not dismayed, for I am your God. I will strengthen you, yes, I will help you, I will uphold you with My righteous right hand (Isaiah 41:10).

But those who wait on the Lord shall renew their strength; they shall mount up with wings like eagles, they shall run and not be weary, they shall walk and not faint (Isaiah 40:31).

The apostle Paul encourages us with this reminder:

I can do all things through Christ who strengthens me (Philippians 4:13).

And finally, the apostle John assures us:

For whatever is born of God overcomes the world. And this is the victory that has overcome the world—our faith (1 John 5:4).

Faith in Christ is the antidote to fear and fatigue. Faith banishes fear and drives out fatigue, leaving peace, confidence, and refreshing in their place.

In Isaiah 60:1, the prophet tells us to *"arise,"* to "get up" psychologically, socially, and physically. His second command to us is to *"shine."* Why? Because "[our] *light has come!"* Notice that our light comes to us from an external source; we do not generate the light ourselves. As Christians, our lives are illuminated by the light of the Lord, which He has given us through His Spirit. The light that shines in our lives is a reflected light. We reflect the light of the Lord God whose Spirit resides in us, just as the moon reflects the light of the sun. Why must we "get up"? Because the time of our illumination has arrived! Jesus said that we are the light of the world and that we are to let our light shine so that others will see our good works (the transformation that the Holy Spirit has made in our lives) and give glory to God the Father. We are to get up so that our light can shine so that other people will be drawn to the Lord by its brightness. We have to get up because, if we don't, our light won't shine, and we will miss the opportunity of being used by God the way He wants to use us as well as miss receiving the fullness of everything He wants to give us.

> # FAITH IN CHRIST IS THE ANTIDOTE TO FEAR AND FATIGUE.

The Hebrew words for "shine" and "light" are essentially the same, with the first referring to the condition of being illuminated and the second to the source or initiator of that illumination. In each instance, the root word also carries connotations of lightning, daybreak, morning, and sun as well as figurative references to light as a divine quality of God Himself and as representing the quality of life that is pleasing to God. We must arise and get up because God is going to shine His light on us—the light of His love, grace, mercy, favor, and blessing—and His purpose is that we shine (as a reflection) His light on others. Only those who have positioned themselves by getting up can expect to experience these blessings from the Lord or to be used by Him in this way to touch the lives of other people. The phrase, *"For your light has come,"* speaks of the anticipation of God's coming to deliver His people and to restore justice to the land. The form of the verb refers to action that has already been completed. So we are not waiting for it to come; it is already here.

Light is a symbol of God's presence, which brings deliverance and blessings. The sun that dispels the gloominess of the night represents God. The presence of God always illuminates a new future for God's people. Whenever God brings light to you, that light dispels the darkness. The devil tries to keep you in darkness—he tries to keep you from getting up—but the moment light comes, it makes you responsible. It changes your environment; it changes everything. When you get up in the middle of the night to go to the bathroom or to get a glass of water, one of the first things you do is flip on the light. The moment you do, your eyes go through 1,000 different adjustments because you have been shrouded in darkness and then suddenly thrust into the light. It's the same way with God. When God brings light into your life, you may fight it at first. You have to adjust to the light, and that is painful for a time because you have become so used to the darkness. Get up! Position yourself to embrace the light, not fight it. When you embrace the light that God shines on you, He will begin to change you. He will turn your life around.

When you get up and change your thinking, when you get up and change your social network, when you get up and change your posture, God says, "My light will shine on you. It will shine on your finances, your family, your relationships, your career, your influence in the community; indeed, on every area of your life." Where the light of God is, there also is the presence of God, and where God is present, there is no lack, no want, no unfulfilled needs. Where God is present, there is no poverty. In every way imaginable, those upon whom the light of God shines, those who have positioned themselves by getting up, are poor no more.

Chapter Five

ARE YOU ISHMAEL, OR ARE YOU ISAAC?

Identity theft is a common and growing problem in today's cyber world. With so much of the business of everyday life being conducted electronically, keeping your personal information secure and private is more challenging today than ever before. Banks, credit unions, insurance companies, credit card companies, hospitals, and any other businesses or organizations that use and store private data on a regular basis spend billions of dollars a year on cyber security to keep that information safe. All it takes is for someone to get hold of your credit card number, social security number, or bank account number, and he can steal your identity and ruin your life.

In the spiritual realm, Satan is also in the identity theft business. He is always at work trying to rob Christian believers of things that are rightfully ours. In particular, he likes to steal our knowledge of our identity in Christ so that we will not know who we are in Him or enjoy all the benefits and blessings that are ours as children of God. Satan cannot change who we are as believers, but he can confuse and blind us to the full knowledge of what it means to be a believer. In this sense, then, Satan deals not so much in identity theft as in identity ignorance. Many believers fail to prosper, fail to grow, fail to experience the fullness of God's blessings, and fail to become all they can be or receive all that is theirs in Christ because they don't know who (or whose) they are.

In Chapter One I asked the question, "Who do you trust?" Now I want to ask you another: "Who are you?" I'm not talking about your family name but about the person you are inside. Who are you, the *real* you deep down inside where no one but God can see? In many ways, we are defined by our character, and character has been defined as who we are when no one is looking. What does your character say about you? Who are you?

A related but equally important question is this: "Do you know *whose* you are?" Who has claim on your life? Your spouse? Your children? Your boss? All of the above? It is certainly true that at certain times and in certain situations all of these people have a legitimate claim to your time and your energy. But who has ultimate claim on your life? Whose are you? Or to put it another way, who do you belong to? These are important questions because the answers you give will determine the direction of your life.

I can hear some of you saying already, "Now wait a minute! I don't belong to anybody! I am a free and self-determining individual. Who says I belong to somebody?" The Bible does, for one. According to the Bible, there are two types of people: those who belong to God and those who belong to the devil, who is the prince of this present world. There are no other options, no middle ground. So I ask you again, who do you belong to?

LIGHT VS. DARKNESS

The Bible uses many symbolic contrasts to reveal the truth about the natural and the spiritual realms. One of the most common and most powerful of these is the contrast between light and darkness. Throughout the Bible, and particularly in the New Testament, the word *light* is used in reference to the Kingdom and people of God. God's Kingdom, or the Kingdom of heaven, is described as a Kingdom of light, and the children of God are those who walk in the light. In contrast, the kingdom of this present world in its sinful rebellion against God is described as a land of darkness and those who dwell in it walk in darkness. So who are you? Are you a child of God or a child of the devil? Are you a child of light or a child of darkness?

This imagery of light and darkness is clearly present in Scripture verses we have already examined in previous chapters and to which I want to return now. Consider once again the words of the prophet Isaiah:

Arise, shine; for your light has come! And the glory of the Lord is risen upon you. For behold, the darkness shall cover the earth, and deep darkness the people; but the Lord will arise over you, and His glory will be seen upon you. The Gentiles shall come to your light, and kings to the brightness of your rising (Isaiah 60:1-3).

Notice the contrast: *darkness* will cover the earth and its people (the children of darkness), but the *light* of God's glory will shine upon His people (the children of light). As the children of light reflect the brilliant radiance of the light of God's glory, many of the children of darkness will be drawn to that light.

Darkness conceals but light reveals. In the darkness, you will stumble around aimlessly and confused with no sense of direction at all; nothing to help you know which way to go. Turn on a light, however, and suddenly the way is clear; the light has scattered the darkness and confusion. The future belongs to those who have the vision to prepare for it, and to be a person of vision you have to walk in the light. We are entering a season when the Lord is going to prosper those who show themselves capable of handling prosperity. I'm not talking just about money and finances, although these are involved, but also about leadership, influence, and training up the next generation in how to walk in the light and in the ways of the Lord. A great harvest of souls is about to come forth and the church must be prepared to receive it. We must be ready to take in the multitudes of people who will be coming from the north, south, east, and west.

In every nation and on every continent of the globe the Holy Spirit is getting millions of people ready to embrace the Kingdom of heaven and the things of God. But He will entrust this harvest to those children of the light who are alive and alert to God's will and purpose, not to those who have attached themselves to the fruitless ways of the world with its darkness and confusion. Claiming the future calls for more than vague hopes, poorly articulated dreams, or even confident assertions alone; claiming the future calls for vision, preparation, and positioning.

THE LIGHT WILL SCATTER DARKNESS AND CONFUSION.

This is why it is so important to know who you are as well as whose you are, for it is only when you know these things that you will be prepared to claim the future. So I ask you once again: "Who are you?" Perhaps it will help if I get a little more specific. Are you an "Ishmael," or are you an "Isaac"? Are you a child of the natural or a child of the Spirit? Are you a child of the earth or a child of heaven? Are you a child of the law or a child of the promise?

Ishmael and Isaac were the first two sons born to Abraham, the father of the nation of Israel. Abraham and his wife Sarah were childless for many years, until long after normal childbearing age. When Abraham was 75, God promised him a son from his own body who would then father a great nation. After many years passed without the promise being fulfilled, Abraham and Sarah began to get a little nervous and decided to take matters into their own hands. Encouraged by Sarah, Abraham fathered a son by Hagar, who was Sarah's handmaiden. He named the boy Ishmael. Although God assured Abraham that He would bless Ishmael and make a great nation of him also, He told Abraham that Ishmael was not the son He had promised years earlier. The "son of promise" was still to come. Finally, when Abraham was 100 and Sarah 90, God's promise was fulfilled when Sarah gave birth to Isaac. Ishmael and Isaac both were sons of Abraham but they had vastly different destinies. While Isaac's descendents became the nation of Israel, Ishmael's descendents gave rise to the Arab nation. And just as Ishmael and Isaac were in conflict with each other in their day, so it remains today between the Arabs and the Jews.

Knowing who you are and whose you are makes all the difference in the world for your future. It all depends on whether you are a son of bondage or a son of liberty; an Ishmael or an Isaac. Here is how the apostle Paul described the difference:

> *For it is written that Abraham had two sons: the one by a bondwoman, the other by a freewoman. But he who was of the bondwoman was born according to the flesh, and he of the freewoman through promise, which things are symbolic. For these are the two covenants: the one from Mount Sinai which gives birth to bondage, which*

is Hagar—for this Hagar is Mount Sinai in Arabia, and corresponds to Jerusalem which now is, and is in bondage with her children—but the Jerusalem above is free, which is the mother of us all....Now we, brethren, as Isaac was, are children of promise. But, as he who was born according to the flesh then persecuted him who was born according to the Spirit, even so it is now. Nevertheless what does the Scripture say? "Cast out the bondwoman and her son, for the son of the bondwoman shall not be heir with the son of the freewoman." So then, brethren, we are not children of the bondwoman but of the free (Galatians 4:22-31).

Ishmael and Isaac both had Abraham for their father, but that is where the similarities ended. Because Hagar, Ishmael's mother, was Sarah's slave (bondwoman), Ishmael was born a slave also, even though he was recognized as Abraham's son. Isaac, on the other hand, was born free because his mother Sarah, Abraham's wife, was a freewoman. This historical reality symbolizes spiritual truth. Ishmael symbolizes the flesh, while Isaac symbolizes the spirit. Ishmael represents all those who are outside the covenant relationship with God. Isaac represents God's covenant people; His chosen people; all those who are children of God by faith and adoption into His family.

Ishmael represents those who are in bondage to the world and its systems; who think and live according to the philosophies and patterns of the world; and whose fortunes rise and fall in line with the ever-changing economic, political, and social orders. They are driven by the flesh, seeking desperately to satisfy every desire in the mistaken belief that the pleasures of this life are all there is, so they had better grab as much as they can while they can.

Isaac represents those whom Christ has set free from the world and its systems, bringing them out of darkness into the light. While "Ishmaels" are driven by the flesh, "Isaacs" are purpose driven and possess a heart to fulfill God's mandate. They are continually learning how to trust God in everything and are committed to following His ways instead of their own. Because "Ishmaels" are self-centered and caught up in the world's way of thinking, God always has to fight with them to bring them in line with His ways. He never has to fight with the "Isaacs," however, because they delight to do His will.

Unfortunately, there are many "Ishmaels" in the church. I'm not talking so much about false believers, those "wolves in sheep's clothing" who try to harass the saints, as I am true believers who somehow have gotten so caught up in the world and its ways that they have taken up an Ishmael mind-set. These are genuine Christians who wonder why they never seem to get ahead, never seem to catch a break, never seem quite able to turn the corner on prosperity, success, and a fulfilled and meaningful life. For them, life always seems to be a little out of sync and they don't know why. They do not understand that because they have been called of God but have been seduced by the world, the world system will no longer work for them. God wants to elevate them to a greater, higher, and better dimension of life. Those who cling to the world's system will continue to be disappointed and ultimately destroyed by deception.

A NEW CURRENCY

God has called all His children, all who claim the name of Christ, to invest in heaven's currency. The currency of heaven is not the Krugerrand or the peso. It is not the lira or the euro. It is not the pound, the sterling, or the dollar. The currency of heaven is faith. Faith is the medium of exchange in which all business between earth and heaven is transacted. Faith is the "monetary standard" upon which all true prosperity and success are based. If you want to be rich in every dimension of life, you must learn how to invest in and use faith, the currency of heaven.

All around us we see evidence of the failure of the world system, of its inability to provide stability, security, and happiness. Although this is true for all of life, it is most clearly evident in the financial and economic realms. Millions of people have lost their jobs and can't find another because few employers are hiring due to the uncertainty of the times. Many have lost their homes, their savings, and their investments. At the time I write this, the number of Americans on food stamps has risen dramatically and more Americans than ever before live officially below the poverty line. The "Ishmaels" of the land have tied their destiny and their fortune so tightly to the world system that they have no control and are at the whim of the economy.

"Isaacs," on the other hand, are unaffected by the instability and uncertainty of the world system because they have invested their destiny and fortune in the currency of heaven, which never fades and never goes into default, evaluation, or depression. If you are an Isaac with your faith fixed on the Lord and trusting in the economy of heaven, you can live and prosper in complete peace and confidence even when there is loss and panic all around you.

> **IF YOU ARE AN ISAAC, YOU CAN LIVE AND PROSPER IN COMPLETE PEACE AND CONFIDENCE.**

During the days of Isaac, Abraham's son of promise, a famine came to the land that was so severe that Isaac was tempted to move to Egypt, where conditions were better. The Lord, however, told him to stay put because his prosperity and welfare did not depend on the whims of nature.

> *There was a famine in the land, besides the first famine that was in the days of Abraham. And Isaac went to Abimelech king of the Philistines, in Gerar. Then the Lord appeared to him and said: "Do not go down to Egypt; live in the land of which I shall tell you. Dwell in this land, and I will be with you and bless you; for to you and your descendants I give all these lands, and I will perform the oath which I swore to Abraham your*

father. And I will make your descendants multiply as the stars of heaven; I will give to your descendants all these lands; and in your seed all the nations of the earth shall be blessed; because Abraham obeyed My voice and kept My charge, My commandments, My statutes, and My laws." So Isaac dwelt in Gerar.… Then Isaac sowed in that land, and reaped in the same year a hundredfold; and the Lord blessed him. The man began to prosper, and continued prospering until he became very prosperous; for he had possessions of flocks and possessions of herds and a great number of servants. So the Philistines envied him (Genesis 26:1-6,12-14).

Isaac obeyed the Lord's command to stay where he was and prospered greatly as a result, in spite of the famine that was ravaging the land. While everyone else was suffering and struggling and going backwards, Isaac kept moving forward and upward, growing in wealth and power every day until he grew so strong that his Philistine neighbors were afraid of him. Isaac was so powerful, in fact, that Abimelech, the local king, asked him to leave the region so they would not feel threatened by him any longer. Abimelech soon regretted his decision when he recognized that it was the Lord who had prospered Isaac.

Then Abimelech came to him from Gerar with Ahuzzath, one of his friends, and Phichol the commander of his army. And Isaac said to them, "Why have you come to me, since you hate me and have sent me away from you?" But they said, "We have certainly

93

seen that the Lord is with you. So we said, 'Let there now be an oath between us, between you and us; and let us make a covenant with you, that you will do us no harm, since we have not touched you, and since we have done nothing to you but good and have sent you away in peace. You are now the blessed of the Lord'" (Genesis 26:26-29).

When God favors His faithful children with the bright lights of His blessings, many who are stumbling in the darkness are drawn to it like moths to a flame. Everybody wants to be where the blessings are flowing, and they flow to the Isaacs of this world, not the Ishmaels. Isaacs refuse to buy into the ups and downs and uncertainties of the world system because they live under a different economy—the economy of heaven. Its currency is faith, and faith wisely and consistently invested returns huge dividends. People want to be a part of something that works, and when the Ishmaels of this world see their "Isaac" neighbors prospering regardless of whatever the economy is doing, they will come and say, "I want to be a part of this. Please tell me how I can 'cash in.'"

Spiritually speaking, the world is shrouded in darkness; most of humanity is trapped in *"deep darkness,"* in the words of Isaiah 60:2. In this context the Hebrew words used for "darkness" refer to spiritual darkness that is impenetrable by any human means or device. In other words, the vast majority of the people of the world are trapped in a darkness of mind and spirit that they have no means of escaping. Most of them are not even aware that they are wandering in the darkness.

If you were to ask them, they would say they can see just fine. But the darkness that blinds their eyes and minds is the darkness of *ignorance* to the truth of the gospel, that there is life and light in Jesus Christ. It is the darkness of *idolatry*, as people in every land and culture devote their time, energy, and resources pursuing things that will never last, never finding the sense of peace and purpose they seek. It is the darkness of *superstition, false doctrine,* and *false worship,* as people who are blind to the truth create gods in their own image and follow the philosophies, principles, and precepts of men.

Jesus said that as His followers we are the light of the world and that we should let our light shine before others so that they will see God's good works and glorify Him. The purpose of the light is to dispel the darkness so that those once blinded by it can see the way that leads them out of bondage. In the Book of Exodus, the Hebrew people, the descendents of Abraham, Isaac, and Jacob, were in bondage to the Egyptians. Yet when the time of their deliverance was at hand, the light of God shone upon them while the rest of the land was in darkness.

Then the Lord said to Moses, "Stretch out your hand toward heaven, that there may be darkness over the land of Egypt, darkness which may even be felt." So Moses stretched out his hand toward heaven, and there was thick darkness in all the land of Egypt three days. They did not see one another; nor did anyone rise from his place for three days. But all the children of Israel had light in their dwellings (Exodus 10:21-23).

The children of God walk in the light as He is in the light, while the rest of the world stumbles in the darkness. It has always been so. We are called to the light so that we can help bring others to the light. We are called to be Isaacs, surrendering our will and purpose to the will and purpose of God, in order to help lead the Ishmaels of the world to the place where God can transform them into Isaacs. Why is it, then, that so many "would-be" Isaacs in the church think and live like Ishmaels? When will believers stand up and take their rightful place as Isaacs? When will *you* lay aside your Ishmael mind-set and live like the Isaac you already are in Christ? You will not until several things happen. First, you must recognize who you are: a child of God and not a child of the world; an Isaac, not an Ishmael. Second, you must recognize that you are the light of the world because the brilliance of the glory of the Lord shines upon you and through you. Third, you must be committed to God's agenda and not your own. Fourth, you must possess a generosity of spirit, mind, and resources, acknowledging that everything you have belongs to God and that He has made you responsible for wise stewardship of everything with which He has entrusted you. Finally, you must assume the position that the Lord has prepared for you so that you may carry out your part in fulfilling God's purpose in this end-time season.

Chapter Six

Do You See the Light?

Some people in Alaska get "SAD" when winter comes. Bright, cheerful, and energetic the rest of the year, at the onset of winter they become depressed, moody, and lethargic. Their mood swing has nothing to do with changes in the temperature or the weather, but everything to do with changes in the *light*. These individuals suffer from a syndrome called "Seasonal Affective Disorder," or "SAD."

Because of its high northerly latitude, Alaska experiences significant changes in the quantity of sunlight it receives, and these changes are tied to the seasons. During the summer, for example, there are some parts of the state where the sun does not set for two or three months at a time, which is why

Alaska is sometimes called the "land of the midnight sun." In the winter, the opposite occurs: the sun never rises above the horizon, or if it does, is only visible for a couple of hours at most before it sets again. As a result, daylight during the winter rarely gets brighter than dusk.

People with Seasonal Affective Disorder become depressed and moody during the winter because they are starved for sunlight. This is more than just an emotional or psychological effect such as when some of us feel "down" on a cloudy day. For people with "SAD" it is also physical; there is a biochemical response to inadequate sunlight. They are fine the rest of the year when there is plenty of sunshine, but they suffer in the winter because there is not enough light.

Although few of us run the risk of suffering from Seasonal Affective Disorder (unless you happen to live in Alaska or somewhere else in the far north latitudes), we are all familiar with milder symptoms of the same kind of thing. Gloomy, overcast skies tend to make us melancholy while bright sunshine and blue skies cheer us, making it easy for us to feel like we are on top of the world. Winter may be gloomy, but there is something about spring, with its return of longer days and more abundant sunlight, that renews hope within the human spirit. I think we humans are connected to the cycle of the seasons physically, emotionally, and psychologically more than we realize. It makes sense, doesn't it? After all, God made the world for man and made man to inhabit the world. That connection is not accidental.

SPIRITUAL "SAD"

The human race was created to walk in the "light" of continual fellowship with God. This is the life Adam and Eve enjoyed in the Garden of Eden, where they walked with God in the cool of the day. Sin changed that idyllic picture. When Adam and Eve disobeyed God, sin entered their lives and plunged them and all succeeding generations into deep spiritual darkness that even today continues to blind most of the people of the world to the truth of the gospel, that there is eternal life and light in Jesus Christ. The world today is afflicted with a spiritual form of Seasonal Affective Disorder: widespread depression and oppression due to inadequate spiritual light...except that in this case the "season" never changes. Spiritually speaking, the world is stuck in perpetual winter.

Grim as this picture is, there is reason for hope. The people who "[walk] *in darkness*" are ready to see a *"great light"*; they who "[dwell] *in the land of the shadow of death"* are ready for a light to shine upon them (Is. 9:2). Although many of them are not consciously aware of it yet, despair over the unending darkness has made them desperate for change. Consequently, they are ripe for salvation. They are ripe for deliverance. They are ripe for liberty. But before this can happen, they must be shown how to look up and set their eyes on the light of the world. Jesus said, *"I am the light of the world. He who follows Me shall not walk in darkness, but have the light of life"* (John 8:12b). But He also said to all who follow Him, *"You are the light of the world. A city that is set on a hill cannot be hidden"* (Matt. 5:14). Jesus is the light of the world, but as Christians we are too because His light and life shine through us. If the darkened world is to see the light of Jesus, we must walk faithfully in His light so that it can dispel the darkness. We are to be lights in the darkness; we are in the world but not of it. This means that our fragrance has to be different; our walk has to be different; our light has to be different. As we saw in the previous chapter, it is the difference between being an Isaac or an Ishmael. Isaacs represent the light because, as citizens of heaven, they are in the world but not of it; the world is not their home. Ishmaels, on the other hand, represent darkness because they are tied to the world and its ways; they are *of* the world as well as in it. When we let our light shine—heaven's light, the light of Christ—it shifts the cosmic order on the earth and breaks the power of spiritual darkness.

> OUR FRAGRANCE, OUR WALK, AND OUR LIGHT HAVE TO BE DIFFERENT FROM THE WORLD'S.

I want to return to the same passage of Scripture in Isaiah 60 that we have examined in previous chapters because it continues to speak into our situation of the light versus the darkness. Consider once more the words of the prophet:

Arise, shine; for your light has come! And the glory of the Lord is risen upon you. For behold, the darkness shall cover the earth, and deep darkness the people; but the Lord will arise over you, and His glory will be seen upon you. The Gentiles shall come to your light, and kings to the brightness of your rising. "Lift up your eyes all around, and see: They all gather together, they come to you; your sons shall come from afar, and your daughters shall be nursed at your side" (Isaiah 60:1-4).

The central theme of these verses and, indeed, of this entire chapter of Isaiah, is restoration. Much of the content of this prophetical book is given over to messages of God's impending judgment on the nations, and especially the nation of Israel, God's own chosen people, because of their wickedness, idolatry, and disobedience. If they persist in their sinfulness, God's judgment will surely fall, but after judgment will come a time of restoration for all the nations, with the people of God leading the way.

Isaiah often speaks prophetically in the past or present tense as though this great restoration has already occurred even though none of it actually came to pass during his lifetime. Much of it is yet to come even in our own day. For example, he says, *"Arise, shine; for your light **has** come"* (Is. 60:1a, emphasis added). He addresses a similar theme much earlier in the book: *"The people who walked in darkness **have** seen a great light; those who dwelt in the land of the shadow of death, upon them a light **has** shined"* (Is. 9:2, emphasis added). Prophetically, this restoration is already fulfilled because it is set in the unshakable and unchanging purpose of God, even though its historical fulfillment did not begin until the birth of Christ hundreds of years later.

The next several verses speak of multiplying the nation, increasing its joy, breaking the yoke of burden and the rod of the oppressor, and burning the implements of war. In the next two verses Isaiah, again speaking in the "prophetic present," clearly links the light that *"has shined"* (verse 2) with the coming of the Messiah:

> *For unto us a Child is born, unto us a Son is given; and the government will be upon His shoulder. And His name will be called Wonderful, Counselor, Mighty God, Everlasting Father, Prince of Peace. Of the increase of His government and peace there will be no end, upon the throne of David and over His kingdom, to order it and establish it with judgment and justice from that time forward, even forever. The zeal of the Lord of hosts will perform this* (Isaiah 9:6-7).

A Child *is* born and a Son *is* given unto us. We understand these verses as clearly referring to the birth of Jesus Christ and to His future eternal reign as King of Kings and Lord of Lords. The name "Jesus," or *Yeshua* in Hebrew, means "Yahweh is salvation." Salvation is the light of grace, mercy, forgiveness, justification, holiness, and wisdom that dispels the darkness of ignorance, sin, sorrow, destruction, and perdition. Spiritual darkness already blankets the earth, but Isaiah promises us that the Lord (Jesus Christ) will *"arise"* as the sun upon Zion. In

Isaiah's day, there was much darkness, but when Jesus Christ came, the *"Sun of Righteousness"* arose *"with healing in His wings"* (Mal. 4:2b) for all the nations of the earth.

WE ARE THE LIGHT

Jesus said that we are the light of the world, but this is true only as we allow His life to fill us and His light to shine upon us and in us and through us. It is His light that we display in our lives, not our own. When we turn to Christ in faith and are born again of the Spirit of God, He who is the *"Sun of Righteousness"* arises over us and imparts His life and light to us so that *"His glory will be seen upon* [us]*"* (Is. 60:2b). Verse 3 says that people of every nation and standing will be drawn to our light. People will have to walk in our light in order to see because the light of Christ in us is the only light that can penetrate the spiritual darkness that has engulfed the world. This is why it is so imperative that we have direction—that we know who we are and where we are going—because the Ishmaels of the world are looking for light in the midst of their darkness.

Being the light of the world means being a beacon of hope to those who are lost in the dark. We must exemplify hope to people distressed by the bleak and dark conditions of their lives. When we let the light of Jesus shine in us, we are saying to the world, "I once was lost but now am found; was blind but now I see." We are saying to the world, "I once was lost in the dark just like you, but Jesus found me and led me into the light. And He can do the same for you."

The children of God reflect the light of God like the moon reflects the light of the sun. As born-again sons and daughters of God, we have His signature upon us; His endorsement, if you will. This should fill us with the supreme confidence that the light we possess is greater than any other light in the world. When people see our light, they will know that we have escaped the darkness, which will encourage them to think, "If they can do it, so can I." Like those on the outside looking longingly through the window at a fabulous and fun party to which they have not been invited, they will see our light, our joy, our peace, and our prosperity, and they will want to have what we have. To those who are stumbling around in the dark, the light of the world says, "You have a chance." If all hell is breaking loose around you, the light of the world says, "You have a chance." If you have cancer, the light of the world says, "You have a chance." If you have diabetes or arthritis, the light of the world says, "You have a chance." You can make it. God can turn your situation around in an instant. Why? Because Jesus Christ, the light of the world, has come to lead out of the darkness all who will choose to follow Him.

In the great restoration that is coming, people of the world will respect the children of God who have positioned themselves for prosperity, aligned themselves with the purposes of God, and who are letting their light shine. People of all nationalities and ethnicities will walk in our light. Muslims will walk in our light; Buddhists will walk in our light; Hare Krishnas will walk in our light; the Church of Scientology will walk in our light; Jehovah's Witnesses will walk in our light. All these and many others will look to us. Why? Because the bright light of God's truth will open their eyes and reveal to them that they are on the wrong path. They will see once and for all that what they have been doing does not work. They also will see the children of God, the children of light, the children of promise, thriving and successful and will realize that we have what they have been looking for all along.

> WHEN THE WORLD SEES THE CHILDREN OF LIGHT THRIVING, THEY WILL WANT WHAT WE HAVE.

Jesus said, *"And I, if I am lifted up from the earth, will draw all peoples to Myself"* (John 12:32). On another occasion He told His disciples, *"Most assuredly, I say to you, he who believes in Me, the works that I do he will do also; and greater works than these he will do, because I go to My Father"* (John 14:12). Jesus, the light of the world, did many great works, yet He says that we who have His light shining in us will do even greater works. Throughout His three-year public ministry, Jesus confined Himself to the provinces of Galilee, Samaria, and Judea, bearing witness to the Kingdom of God yet never venturing more than 150 miles from the place of His birth. But He told His disciples, *"You shall be witnesses to Me in Jerusalem, and in all Judea and Samaria, **and to the end of the earth**"* (Acts 1:8b, emphasis added). As children of the light, we will bear His light to people and places He never went to. In these end times, the Lord is positioning His people to shine brightly in a dark world and draw all people to Himself. He is setting the stage for the great day when at the name of Jesus every knee will bow and every tongue confess that Jesus Christ is Lord (Phil. 2:10-11).

Everyday people will come: laborers, waitresses, secretaries. Professional people will come: doctors, nurses, lawyers, teachers. Businesspeople will come. Theologians will come. Scientists and philosophers will come. Soldiers and sailors will come. Rich and poor, young and old will come. People of rank and of no rank will come. People well-known and people unknown will come. Hollywood celebrities and TV stars will come. Heads of state will come: kings, presidents, prime ministers. Government leaders will come: senators, representatives, governors, mayors. Everywhere, people will come, from every continent and every nation on the face of the earth, looking for salvation, hope, and a brighter tomorrow: England, Germany, France, USA, Belgium, Canada, Mexico, Australia, Sweden, Russia, Iran, Iraq, Venezuela, Pakistan, Cuba, Tanzania, Nigeria, Italy, China, Japan, North Korea, South Korea, Vietnam, Laos, Cambodia, India, Afghanistan, Indonesia, Malaysia, Brazil, Argentina, Peru, Bolivia, Venezuela, Colombia. Together they will bow their knees at the foot of the cross and testify as one mighty voice that "Jesus Christ is Lord!"

THE ABSOLUTE TRUTH

There is a crisis of truth in our society today. In the minds of many, there is no such thing as "absolute truth"; rather, truth is what we make it to be, and it can change from one person to the next. What you consider truth may not be truth for me, and vice versa. With this kind of mind-set, many people can hold two or more contradictory beliefs simultaneously and see no conflict. If truth is relative, there is no absolute standard by which to measure, and truth becomes a very private thing; truth is whatever works for you.

This is where persistent and pervasive spiritual blindness has brought us: an "anything goes" philosophy that has grown out of mankind's well-intentioned but misguided search for relevance, tolerance, and meaning. People need to know the truth whether they realize it or not. They need to know that there is an absolute, rock-solid standard upon which they can anchor their lives, their hopes, and their dreams, a standard that can help them make sense of a senseless world.

Contrary to the increasingly common view of many people today, there *is* a standard of absolute truth, and His name is Jesus. He could not have been any plainer about this than when He said, *"I am the way, the truth, and the life. No one comes to the Father except through Me"* (John 14:6). In another place He said, *"If you abide in My word, you are My disciples indeed. And you shall know the truth, and the truth shall make you free"* (John 8:31b-32). People trapped in the bondage of sin, darkness, and moral and ethical relativism need to know that there is freedom in the truth. The truth is Jesus Christ, and He never changes: *"Jesus Christ is the same yesterday, today, and forever"* (Heb. 13:8).

As we have already seen, light in the Bible is associated with truth and life, and darkness with deception and death. As Christians, we are to be those who *"walk in the light as He is in the light"* (1 John 1:7a). With the Holy Spirit's indwelling presence, we are brightly shining beacons of the Lord in the world and we must not hide our light under a bushel basket.

So let me ask you: "Do you see the light?" Even more importantly, do others see the light in you? Do they see it in the way you walk, in the way you talk, in the way you dress, and in the way you carry yourself? Do they see the light of Christ in the way you treat your children and in the way you treat your spouse? Do they see it in the workplace, in the attitude you take toward your work? Do they see it in the way you treat and relate to your coworkers? Do they see it in the respect and honor you give to your boss and others who are in authority over you? Do they see the light of Christ in the honor and respect you show to all people, and especially those who are under your authority? Do they see it in the way you handle your finances and in the way you spend your money? Do they see it in the way you refuse to wear the label of "loser" or "victim," but walk, talk, and carry yourself like the winner you are?

If you know the truth and abide in it, you will prosper; that is a biblical promise. But prosperity has to do with so much more than just money. When the Lord prospers you, you will walk in freedom, knowledge, grace, confidence, assurance, peace, joy, and provision for every need. Prosperity does not mean being in the position to have everything you have ever dreamed of having nearly as much as it means God positioning you for the purpose and dream He has had for you since before the foundation of the world. There is no greater prosperity than being in the center of God's will and fulfilling His eternal purpose for you in His plan for the world. This is the life Jesus was referring to when He said, *"I have come that they may have life, and that they may have it more abundantly"* (John 10:10b).

> THERE IS NO GREATER PROSPERITY THAN BEING IN THE CENTER OF GOD'S WILL.

If your life shines in this way, people will be drawn to you from every direction. They will see your blessedness, the favor of God resting upon you, and His spiritual power at work in you, and they will want what you have. As the children of God walk in the light of God's favor and prosperity, many people who are stumbling around in the darkness will see His light in us and run toward it, and we will begin to see souls saved in massive and epic proportions. This is why the Lord has got to get us ready, for the wheels are now in motion. We must be prepared because the harvest is already underway. One report, for example, reveals that Muslims are now converting to Christ at the average rate of 1600 *per day*, many of them after receiving a dream or vision of Christ. The Spirit of God is mightily at work in Asia, Africa, and Latin America. We need to pray that He begins to work just as mightily in the nations of the West, including the United States.

Isaiah 60:4 says, *"Lift up your eyes all around, and see: They all gather together, they come to you; your sons shall come from afar, and your daughters shall be nursed at your side."* In other words, open your eyes and see the great harvest of souls that awaits you; the great crowd of sons and daughters who have been and will be attracted to your light. Some of them you will already know—friends, neighbors, and coworkers—but many you will not. These will come because they have been drawn irresistibly to the light of Christ shining in your life. And they will say to you, "Whatever you have in your life, I want it, and I won't stop until I get it." They will see the living Christ revealed in your life and will find the Savior they did not even know they were looking for.

To be "poor no more" does not mean being rich in the things of the world. Many wealthy people have more money than they know what to do with, yet are empty and destitute in spirit, poverty-stricken in the things that matter most. Rather, to be "poor no more" means to be rich in the things of God: filled with His presence, infused with His purpose, empowered by His Spirit, and illuminated by the light of His glory.

Chapter Seven

GET READY TO SHINE

There are many situations that arise in life that cause us to feel insecure: war; dangerous weather conditions such as hurricanes, tornadoes, or floods; disease epidemics; violent crime waves; economic downturns or reversals. These are just a few, but whatever the root cause, the insecurity and fear that result affect every area of our experiences, from our home life to our workplace and from our relationships to our pocketbooks. Perhaps no single cause creates more fear and uncertainty and affects more people across a wider scale of influence than does an ailing economy. People who have trouble making ends meet even during the best of times are hit especially hard whenever the economy takes a dive. Economic uncertainty breeds fear, which can lead to widespread social unrest and spark an upsurge in rash and

POOR NO MORE

even criminal behavior. These responses are amplified when several crises hit over a short period of time.

Christian economist Larry Bates has identified five powerful, dangerous, and unstoppable forces that have hit the U.S. economy within the past several years:

1. The banking crisis of 2008–2009. This is the tenth banking crisis in the United States since the founding of our nation over 200 years ago. (The others occurred in the years 1797, 1819, 1837, 1857, 1873, 1893, 1907, 1929, and 1987.)

2. The crisis of federal debts and deficits. The years 2009–2011 saw a greater increase in the U.S. deficit than in all the previous years of our nation's history *combined*.

3. The crisis of business and personal debt. Levels of both business and personal debt have never been higher.

4. The crisis of recession and depression. The recession of the past several years is the worst Americans have experienced since the Great Depression of the 1930s, and at the time of this writing there were renewed fears of a "double dip" recession.

5. The crisis of massive renewed inflation. Prices keep going up while the buying power of the average American keeps going down, until today more Americans than ever before officially live below the poverty line.[1]

112

Negative economic drivers such as these stir up unrest, fear, and insecurity that range far beyond worries over money matters alone. In the minds of many, economic uncertainty threatens to destabilize the very fabric and structure of society itself. It is especially during times such as these that the people of God must keep their eyes fixed on Christ, the Light of the world. We must stand firm and confident in our Lord in order to shine His light before a fearful world and show them that there is a stable foundation upon which to stand even when the institutions of man appear to be crumbling.

GOD'S KINGDOM IS GREATER

If there is one thing that the Bible makes perfectly clear, it is that the Kingdom of God is never affected by the ups and downs and changing fortunes of the kingdoms of the world. Earthly kingdoms come and go and empires rise and fall, but the Kingdom of God stands forever. It is immovable and unshakable, and even the greatest of human kingdoms pale in comparison to it. As Creator, God owns all things, and He can transfer anything He wishes into the hands of anyone He chooses according to whatever pleases Him. The Bible contains numerous accounts of such transfers, particularly transfers of wealth, often under circumstances that appeared unlikely or even impossible to human eyes. Let's consider a few examples:

> *Then Elisha said, "Hear the word of the Lord. Thus says the Lord: 'Tomorrow about this time a seah of fine*

flour shall be sold for a shekel, and two seahs of barley for a shekel, at the gate of Samaria.'" So an officer on whose hand the king leaned answered the man of God and said, "Look, if the Lord would make windows in heaven, could this thing be?" And he said, "In fact, you shall see it with your eyes, but you shall not eat of it." Now there were four leprous men at the entrance of the gate; and they said to one another, "Why are we sitting here until we die? If we say, 'We will enter the city,' the famine is in the city, and we shall die there. And if we sit here, we die also. Now therefore, come, let us surrender to the army of the Syrians. If they keep us alive, we shall live; and if they kill us, we shall only die." And they rose at twilight to go to the camp of the Syrians; and when they had come to the outskirts of the Syrian camp, to their surprise no one was there. For the Lord had caused the army of the Syrians to hear the noise of chariots and the noise of horses—the noise of a great army; so they said to one another, "Look, the king of Israel has hired against us the kings of the Hittites and the kings of the Egyptians to attack us!" Therefore they arose and fled at twilight, and left the camp intact—their tents, their horses, and their donkeys—and they fled for their lives. And when these lepers came to the outskirts of the camp, they went into one tent and ate and drank, and carried from it silver and gold and clothing, and went and hid them; then they came back and entered another tent, and carried some from there also, and went and hid it.

Then they said to one another, "We are not doing right. This day is a day of good news, and we remain silent. If we wait until morning light, some punishment will come upon us. Now therefore, come, let us go and tell the king's household." So they went and called to the gatekeepers of the city, and told them, saying, "We went to the Syrian camp, and surprisingly no one was there, not a human sound—only horses and donkeys tied, and the tents intact." And the gatekeepers called out, and they told it to the king's household inside. So the king arose in the night and said to his servants, "Let me now tell you what the Syrians have done to us. They know that we are hungry; therefore they have gone out of the camp to hide themselves in the field, saying, 'When they come out of the city, we shall catch them alive, and get into the city.'" And one of his servants answered and said, "Please, let several men take five of the remaining horses which are left in the city. Look, they may either become like all the multitude of Israel that are left in it; or indeed, I say, they may become like all the multitude of Israel left from those who are consumed; so let us send them and see." Therefore they took two chariots with horses; and the king sent them in the direction of the Syrian army, saying, "Go and see." And they went after them to the Jordan; and indeed all the road was full of garments and weapons which the Syrians had thrown away in their haste. So the messengers returned and told the king. Then the people went out and plundered the tents of the Syrians. So a seah of fine flour was sold for a shekel, and two seahs of barley for a shekel, according to the word of the Lord (2 Kings 7:1-16).

This is a long passage, but we need to take notice of several important things. First of all, on the surface of things, to all appearances, Israel's situation was dire. The city of Samaria, the capital city of the northern kingdom of Israel, was surrounded by the Syrian army and under siege. Food was all but gone and the people inside the city were beginning to starve. Because the necessities of life were scarce, inflation was rampant and prices for basic goods were sky-high. The Syrian army was large, powerful, and seemingly invincible. The Israelites had a major crisis on their hands. Even when the prophet Elisha announced that the crisis would break in favor of the Israelites, it sounded too good to be true. But that is exactly what happened. Against all odds and human expectations, the Lord Himself stirred up fear in the Syrian army that they were about to be attacked by a greater force, and they fled in panic, leaving everything behind. Once the Israelites in the city realized what had happened, they had a field day going out and claiming the spoils for themselves: tents, horses, donkeys, silver, gold, fine clothing, etc. This was much more than a simple transfer of wealth; God also delivered them from a very dangerous situation. Literally overnight, He turned their situation around.

A similar account is recorded in the Book of 2 Chronicles, this time involving the southern kingdom of Judah and their king, Jehoshaphat. This too is a long passage, but it is necessary to get the full effect of what happened.

It happened after this that the people of Moab with the people of Ammon, and others with them besides the Ammonites, came to battle against Jehoshaphat. Then some came and told Jehoshaphat, saying, "A great multitude is coming against you from beyond the sea, from Syria; and they are in Hazazon Tamar" (which is En Gedi). And Jehoshaphat feared, and set himself to seek the Lord, and proclaimed a fast throughout all Judah. So Judah gathered together to ask help from the Lord; and from all the cities of Judah they came to seek the Lord. Then Jehoshaphat stood in the assembly of Judah and Jerusalem, in the house of the Lord, before the new court, and said: "O Lord God of our fathers, are You not God in heaven, and do You not rule over all the kingdoms of the nations, and in Your hand is there not power and might, so that no one is able to withstand You? Are You not our God, who drove out the inhabitants of this land before Your people Israel, and gave it to the descendants of Abraham Your friend forever? And they dwell in it, and have built You a sanctuary in it for Your name, saying, 'If disaster comes upon us—sword, judgment, pestilence, or famine—we will stand before this temple and in Your presence (for Your name is in this temple), and cry out to You in our affliction, and You will hear and save.' And now, here are the people of Ammon, Moab, and Mount Seir—whom You would not let Israel invade when they came out of the land of Egypt, but they turned from them and did not destroy them—here they are, rewarding us by coming to throw us out of Your possession which You have given us to inherit. O our God, will You not judge them? For we have no power against this great multitude that is coming against us; nor do we know what to do, but our eyes are upon You."

Now all Judah, with their little ones, their wives, and their children, stood before the Lord. Then the Spirit of the Lord came upon Jahaziel the son of Zechariah, the son of Benaiah, the son of Jeiel, the son of Mattaniah, a Levite of the sons of Asaph, in the midst of the assembly. And he said, "Listen, all you of Judah and you inhabitants of Jerusalem, and you, King Jehoshaphat! Thus says the Lord to you: 'Do not be afraid nor dismayed because of this great multitude, for the battle is not yours, but God's. Tomorrow go down against them. They will surely come up by the Ascent of Ziz, and you will find them at the end of the brook before the Wilderness of Jeruel. You will not need to fight in this battle. Position yourselves, stand still and see the salvation of the Lord, who is with you, O Judah and Jerusalem!' Do not fear or be dismayed; tomorrow go out against them, for the Lord is with you." And Jehoshaphat bowed his head with his face to the ground, and all Judah and the inhabitants of Jerusalem bowed before the Lord, worshiping the Lord. Then the Levites of the children of the Kohathites and of the children of the Korahites stood up to praise the Lord God of Israel with voices loud and high.

So they rose early in the morning and went out into the Wilderness of Tekoa; and as they went out, Jehoshaphat stood and said, "Hear me, O Judah and you inhabitants of Jerusalem: Believe in the Lord your God, and you shall be established; believe His prophets, and you shall prosper." And when he had consulted with the people, he appointed those who should sing to the Lord, and who should praise the beauty of holiness, as they went out before the army and were saying: "Praise the Lord, for His mercy endures forever." Now when they began to sing and to praise, the Lord set ambushes against the people of Ammon, Moab, and Mount Seir, who had come against Judah; and they were defeated. For the people of Ammon and Moab stood up against the inhabitants of Mount Seir to utterly kill and destroy them. And when they had made an end of the inhabitants of Seir, they helped to destroy one another. So when Judah came to a place overlooking the wilderness, they looked toward the multitude; and there were their dead bodies, fallen on the earth. No one had escaped. When Jehoshaphat and his people came to take away their spoil, they found among them an abundance of valuables on the dead bodies, and precious jewelry, which they stripped off for themselves, more than they could carry away; and they were three days gathering the spoil because there was so much (2 Chronicles 20:1-25).

Jehoshaphat was a righteous king who followed God faithfully throughout his reign. When Judah was threatened by three neighboring nations, Jehoshaphat did the right thing: He took the matter to God in prayer and in doing so set an example for the nation. The king praised God's greatness and acknowledged that He was their God and that they were His people. In great humility he confessed their inability to stand against the forces that had come to destroy them and asked the Lord to show them what to do and to deliver them. Once again, God turned their situation around without a fight. Rather than attacking Jehoshaphat and his people, the armies of the three opposing nations attacked each other and wiped each other out. Jehoshaphat and the people of Judah knew that they faced a hopeless situation, humanly speaking, but they trusted in God for their deliverance. God defeated their enemies and the people went out to collect the spoils. Because there was so much, it took them three days to gather it all.

In both of these examples, the people of God prospered when they positioned themselves to receive God's provision rather than trying to take care of themselves in their own strength. Sometimes, as with the prophet Elisha in the first passage, all it takes is one faithful person to be in position before God in order for everyone to be blessed. It seems as though none of the people of Samaria, including the king, was expecting divine deliverance. They were pessimistic about their chances and saw no way out. Elisha, on the other hand, always saw things from God's perspective, and because Elisha was faithful, God brought deliverance to the entire city. In the second example, Jehoshaphat and the people of

Jerusalem collectively looked to God for their deliverance, and He honored their faith and answered their request.

The point I am making here is that the true path to prosperity in all of its various forms lies in trusting the Lord rather than relying on our own wisdom, strength, or resources. One reason the world as a whole is in such a sorry state today is because people refuse to look to God. They refuse to acknowledge Him as God and they reject His ways. Consequently, they continue to wander in spiritual darkness, with the vast majority of the people of the world living in destitute and desperate circumstances, quite often due in large part to their being victimized by the rich. This is why the world stands in desperate need of people of God who have positioned themselves to be lights to show the rest of the world that there is a better way.

> THE TRUE PATH TO PROSPERITY LIES IN TRUSTING THE LORD.

I want to give one more example to drive the lesson home and show that even unbelievers can share in God's blessings when they come under the influence of a child of God who is in position to let his or her light shine. In this example, that shining light is Joseph. You may recall that Joseph was sold into slavery by his jealous brothers and ended up in Egypt as a slave of Potiphar, Pharaoh's captain of the guard. Because

Joseph always sought to position himself in the center of God's will wherever he was, God prospered him. He became head of Potiphar's household until Potiphar's wife falsely accused him of assaulting her, and he was put in prison. Even in prison, however, he rose to the top, being entrusted by the warden with the care of all the other prisoners. Then finally came the time when Joseph interpreted a troubling dream for Pharaoh, a dream predicting prosperity followed by famine, and Pharaoh promoted Joseph to second-in-command over all Egypt. From this position, Joseph administered affairs wisely to protect the people during seven years of famine. Our scriptural example picks up in the middle of the famine.

> *Now there was no bread in all the land; for the famine was very severe, so that the land of Egypt and the land of Canaan languished because of the famine. And Joseph gathered up all the money that was found in the land of Egypt and in the land of Canaan, for the grain which they bought; and Joseph brought the money into Pharaoh's house. So when the money failed in the land of Egypt and in the land of Canaan, all the Egyptians came to Joseph and said, "Give us bread, for why should we die in your presence? For the money has failed." Then Joseph said, "Give your livestock, and I will give you bread for your livestock, if the money is gone." So they brought their livestock to Joseph, and Joseph gave them bread in exchange for the horses, the flocks, the cattle of the herds, and for the donkeys. Thus he fed them with bread in exchange for all their livestock that*

year. When that year had ended, they came to him the next year and said to him, "We will not hide from my lord that our money is gone; my lord also has our herds of livestock. There is nothing left in the sight of my lord but our bodies and our lands. Why should we die before your eyes, both we and our land? Buy us and our land for bread, and we and our land will be servants of Pharaoh; give us seed, that we may live and not die, that the land may not be desolate."

Then Joseph bought all the land of Egypt for Pharaoh; for every man of the Egyptians sold his field, because the famine was severe upon them. So the land became Pharaoh's. And as for the people, he moved them into the cities, from one end of the borders of Egypt to the other end. Only the land of the priests he did not buy; for the priests had rations allotted to them by Pharaoh, and they ate their rations which Pharaoh gave them; therefore they did not sell their lands. Then Joseph said to the people, "Indeed I have bought you and your land this day for Pharaoh. Look, here is seed for you, and you shall sow the land. And it shall come to pass in the harvest that you shall give one-fifth to Pharaoh. Four-fifths shall be your own, as seed for the field and for your food, for those of your households and as food for your little ones." So they said, "You have saved our lives; let us find favor in the sight of my lord, and we will be Pharaoh's servants." And Joseph made it a law over the land of Egypt to this day, that Pharaoh should have

*one-fifth, except for the land of the priests only, which
did not become Pharaoh's* (Genesis 47:13-26).

The Egyptian people who came to Joseph for help
during the famine were not part of God's "chosen people,"
the Hebrews. In fact, few if any of them either acknowledged
or worshiped the one true God. Joseph did, however, and
God had positioned him to be as a light for the Egyptians
in the darkness of famine, starvation, and want. Because
they came to where the light was shining, they received
everything they needed even when all the nations around
them were suffering.

In this example, we could liken the people of the world
today to those of ancient Egypt in Joseph's day. Now, as then,
people in darkness need a shining light to show them the
way out of their poverty (both material and spiritual), their
hopelessness, and their lives that have no future apart from
Christ. In these things, as always, God is looking for those of
His people who are willing and ready to position themselves
to be those lights in the darkness.

Whenever God gets ready to do a mighty work in
the Earth, He always looks for people who will surrender
themselves to be His instruments. So let me ask you: *"Are
you ready to shine?"*

ABUNDANCE IS COMING

Let's return briefly to chapter 60 of the Book of Isaiah.
In previous chapters we have considered the first four verses.
Now I want us to examine verse 5:

Then you shall see and become radiant, and your heart shall swell with joy; because the abundance of the sea shall be turned to you, the wealth of the Gentiles shall come to you (Isaiah 60:5).

You will recall that verse 1 commands us to arise and shine because our light has come and the glory of the Lord has risen upon us. Verse 2 says that although darkness covers the earth, the glory of God will be seen upon His people. Verses 3 and 4 tell us that people from all walks of life will be drawn to the brightness of our rising. Verse 5 tells us that

GET READY TO SHINE!

we *"shall see and become radiant"* and that our hearts *"shall swell with joy."* Why? Because the abundance of the sea and the wealth of the Gentiles shall come to us.

If you're serious about seeing your life turned around, your relationships transformed, and your future no longer tied down and hindered by the baggage of your past; if you are serious about seizing your destiny and becoming everything God wants you to be; if you are serious enough to get up physically, mentally, and socially and to position yourself as a light in the darkness, I have one thing to say to you: *Get ready to shine!*

If you're serious, then God is saying to you, "You are going to see for yourself in this season how I will turn your life and situation completely around." The Bible says that the saints of the Lord are destined to reign with Him in the world to come. One of the purposes of the Christian life is to groom us and prepare us for that destiny. As we get up, as we position ourselves, as we prove ourselves faithful with little things, He will entrust us with bigger and greater things. We hear so much talk in the church about prosperity in the context of money and material wealth that it is easy to forget that the abundance and prosperity mentioned in these verses and throughout the Bible is far deeper, broader, and higher than material possessions. If your idea of prosperity and abundance focuses on money alone, then you are thinking too small. Of course, there is no poverty in the Kingdom of God; no recession, depression, inflation, debt, deficit, or any other kind of economic malady. There is no lack in God's Kingdom. Abundance of every kind characterizes the Kingdom of God: health, destiny, purpose, joy and peace; in short, everything that we as humans have been dreaming of and striving for every since sin cut off our first ancestors from these things in the Garden of Eden. That which our original "parents" lost in Eden God is getting ready to restore, and it will come first to His children who have positioned themselves by faith to receive it and to shine the light of truth—the light of Christ—into the darkness so that people from every nation can come and take part.

So get ready to shine. The entire world is watching for our radiance. They want to see the brightness of our rising.

1. Larry Bates, *The New Economic Disorder*, rev. ed. (Lake Mary, FL: Excel Books, A Strang Company, 2009).

Chapter Eight

FOUR PILLARS OF TRUE WEALTH

Throughout this book I have stressed the importance of preparation and positioning if you wish to be in line to enter into the fullness of everything God has destined for you. I have talked about how you must get your act together psychologically; to have the right mind-set. I have talked about how you must disconnect socially from everyone who would hold you back from your destiny because of his or her own limited vision and connect to anyone who will help you reach it. I have talked about the importance of changing your posture, of adopting the thought processes, appearance, and behavior of the person of destiny you want to be.

All of this means that you must be proactive with your life rather than reactive; you must initiate action and take deliberate steps rather than simply react to circumstances. You have to get up physically, mentally, and socially. If you want your life to change, you must change your thinking, your behavior, and the way you spend your time, money, and other resources. You also must reevaluate the company you keep.

Lastly, I have stressed the importance of understanding that as Christians we are the light of the world, with the light of the living Christ shining in each of us. Christ has called us to be lights in the darkness that covers the world, and as His glory shines brightly in us, many of those who are stumbling in the darkness will be drawn to our light.

Proactive preparation and positioning are extremely important because success in life rarely is achieved by accident. If you want to reach a particular destination, you must plan your route carefully. You can't simply jump into your car and head off in any direction you please. Success in any endeavor means not only knowing where you want to go but also knowing how you plan to get there.

In the course of our journey through these pages we have used the first several verses of Isaiah chapter 60 as our guide. In the context of these verses I have discussed the importance of embracing our role as lights in the darkness in these end times so that, we will be in position to receive from the Lord the great end-time transference of wealth that is coming. This wealth is not necessarily or even primarily material in nature, but is much wider than that, encompassing everything—physical, mental, emotional, psychological, and spiritual—that comprises what Jesus called the "abundant" life. Truly, the greatest wealth of all to be transferred is the priceless wealth of human souls that will depart the kingdom of darkness and enter the Kingdom of light in a great end-time harvest.

Many people have a narrow, incomplete, or erroneous idea of wealth. Wealth is more than just having a lot of money or a lot of stuff. True wealth is defined more by the nature and quality of what you have rather than the quantity, and it transcends the issue of money and material possessions. Unlike false wealth, which creates the illusion of prosperity but can disappear literally overnight when a sudden reversal occurs, true wealth has a lasting quality as well as the ability to perpetuate itself. In other words, true wealth consists of things of value that do not fade or pass away over time and which by their nature produce more wealth and are protected from reversal and loss.

With this in mind, I want to discuss briefly the four pillars of true wealth: capitalization, allocation, appropriation, and preservation.

PILLAR #1: CAPITAL

Capital refers to accumulated goods devoted to the production of other goods or for the production of income. In other words, capital involves the funds or other resources necessary to do what we need to do. Businesses, for example, need capital, an infusion of money to cover start-up costs and operational expenses until they begin turning a profit. This is why people who wish to start a business often seek partners or investors who will provide the needed funds to launch the business. Additional capital is then needed periodically for investments as well as for the expansion of the business, such as opening new branches or purchasing other businesses as subsidiaries.

Although the word *capital* is most familiar to us in the context of the business and financial worlds, the concept of capital applies to any arena of life, to any situation where we wish to move from where we are to where we want to be. In other words, if you know where you want to go and you have a plan for taking you there, making the journey between the two will require the investment of capital, whether it be time, money, energy, labor, discipline, or all of these in various measure. For example, you may desire a better job with higher pay, better benefits, and an upwardly mobile career path, but have determined that in order to qualify for it you need more education. That better job is your desired destination, and more education is the path to get you there. Traveling that path, however, will require a capital investment of money to pay for school, time for attending classes and doing homework, and the discipline to study hard. You invest the necessary capital now in the hope and expectation of getting abundant returns on your investment later.

The concept of capital investment is just as applicable to the spiritual life as it is to the physical. Spiritual progress and spiritual breakthrough acquire investment and availability of spiritual capital. After His resurrection but before He ascended to His Father, Jesus commissioned His body, the church, to the assignment of global evangelism, but He did not leave us without resources—capital—for getting the job done. He said:

> All authority has been given to Me in heaven and on earth. Go therefore and make disciples of all the nations, baptizing them in the name of the Father and of the Son and of the Holy Spirit, teaching them to observe all things that I have commanded you; and lo, I am with you always, even to the end of the age (Matthew 28:18b-20).

THE LORD HAS INVESTED IN US ALL THE CAPITAL WE NEED TO CARRY OUT HIS WILL.

Jesus commissioned us as His people to *"make disciples of all the nations,"* and the capital that He has invested for completing this task is Himself: *"I am with you always."* His presence in the Person of the Holy Spirit leads us and empowers us to fulfill our commission:

> But you shall receive power when the Holy Spirit has come upon you; and you shall be witnesses to Me in

Jerusalem, and in all Judea and Samaria, and to the end of the earth (Acts 1:8).

If this is true, then why do so many churches and Christians seem powerless when it comes to reaching the world with the gospel? I believe one reason is that the poverty mind-set that afflicts so many people, including many Christians, in the everyday affairs of work, home, and money has infiltrated into the church. Many Christians who assume that they will always be poor in the natural realm assume that the same is true in the spiritual realm. They either have forgotten or simply do not truly believe that the Lord has invested in His people all the capital they need to carry out His will. He has equipped us to be successful in everything He desires us to do and be, and we need to claim that and live by it. The apostle Paul said, *"And my God shall supply all your need according to His riches in glory by Christ Jesus"* (Phil. 4:19). John expressed a similar idea when he wrote:

Now this is the confidence that we have in Him, that if we ask anything according to His will, He hears us. And if we know that He hears us, whatever we ask, we know that we have the petitions that we have asked of Him (1 John 5:14-15).

The point I am making here is that whatever God has called you to do, whatever dream He has placed in your heart, whatever path He is leading you down, whether in the natural realm of daily living or in the spiritual realm of walking with Him, He has given you all the "capital" you need to do it.

Pillar #2: Allocation

The second pillar of true wealth is wealth allocation. This means that when God transfers wealth to His people, He allocates it, or distributes it, according to His will, our abilities and preparedness, and the specific calling He has given to each of us. In other words, God will allocate to you whatever wealth and resources, both physical and spiritual, that you need to fulfill the specific call He has placed in your life. He is the giver, we are the receivers, and He decides what to give us according to our needs. As Paul informs us:

> *There are diversities of gifts, but the same Spirit. There are differences of ministries, but the same Lord. And there are diversities of activities, but it is the same God who works all in all. But the manifestation of the Spirit is given to each one for the profit of all:... But one and the same Spirit works all these things, distributing to each one individually as He wills* (1 Corinthians 12:4-7,11).

God is purposeful in everything He does; there is nothing random in His actions or haphazard about His words. He never speaks just to have something to say and never does anything without a reason. So when the Spirit of God distributes the gifts of the Spirit and transfers the "wealth of the Gentiles" to the people of God, *"to each one individually as He wills,"* He does not do so willy-nilly but with deliberate purpose and according to our individual capabilities.

Jesus illustrates this principle in His parable of the talents:

For the kingdom of heaven is like a man traveling to a far country, who called his own servants and delivered his goods to them. And to one he gave five talents, to another two, and to another one, to each according to his own ability; and immediately he went on a journey (Matthew 25:14-15).

Notice that each servant received *"talents"* from his master *"according to his own ability."* Each servant was a receiver who had no right to expect or demand anything from his master; the master alone determined the nature and magnitude of the talents each servant received. He knew the capabilities of each servant and allocated his goods accordingly.

This is where preparation and positioning come into play. Although God allocates gifts, wealth, and resources according to His own will, the Bible also says that He delights to give good things to His people. The more you prepare, the more you get up, the more you let your light shine—in other words, the more you show yourself faithful—the more you will position yourself to receive greater allocation.

PILLAR #3: APPROPRIATION

After capitalization and allocation, the third pillar of true wealth is wealth appropriation. Appropriation means to put your allocation to good use. I'm sure we have all heard at one time or another of someone being accused of "misappropriation of funds." This means that the person made improper or dishonest use of funds allocated to him or her for a specific purpose. Proper appropriation of your allocation is very important. Whatever God has entrusted you with He expects you to use for His glory and other people's good, and He has given you the wisdom and the capability of doing so. And He will hold you accountable.

Continuing with Jesus' parable of the talents, we see examples of both appropriation and misappropriation:

> *Then he who had received the five talents went and traded with them, and made another five talents. And likewise he who had received two gained two more also. But he who had received one went and dug in the ground, and hid his lord's money* (Matthew 25:16-18).

> **WHAT GOD HAS GIVEN TO YOU, HE EXPECTS YOU TO USE FOR HIS GLORY AND OTHER PEOPLE'S GOOD.**

The first two servants understood the principle of wealth appropriation. Wasting no time, they got down to business and through wise trading doubled their resources. When was the last time you got a 100% return on your investment? These servants were prepared, they were in position, they knew what their master expected of them, and they were committed to doing his will. It doesn't matter that the first servant began and ended with more talents than the second servant. What matters is that each servant began with an allocation that matched his abilities and made full appropriation of his allocation in full accordance with his abilities.

Unlike the first two servants, the third servant misappropriated his allocation. He did not steal it, embezzle it, gamble it away, or lose it through foolish investment. He simply did nothing except to hide his allocation to keep it safe for his master's return. Misappropriation does not always mean doing something wrong with your allocation; it can also mean *not* doing something *right* with it, such as doing nothing, when you have the opportunity and the ability to do otherwise. This servant had the same potential to succeed as did the first two. Remember, God never acts without purpose. As with the first two, the master gave this third servant one talent *"according to his own ability."* And, like his two fellow servants, this servant had the wisdom and the ability to double his assets. His problem was that he did not understand the principle of appropriation. He let fear of losing his allocation paralyze him into inaction, and he thought it was safer simply to hide it away.

Appropriation has to do with stewardship. A steward is a person who has been given management responsibility of someone else's property, resources, or assets and is accountable to the owner for his or her appropriation of those assets. As children of God we are stewards of all that He has allocated to us and are responsible to Him for our use of them. If we want to be entrusted with a greater transference of wealth, we must prove ourselves faithful with what God has already given us. Jesus makes this point in another parable about servants:

Who then is that faithful and wise steward, whom his master will make ruler over his household, to give them their portion of food in due season? Blessed is that servant whom his master will find so doing when he comes. Truly, I say to you that he will make him ruler over all that he has. But if that servant says in his heart, "My master is delaying his coming," and begins to beat the male and female servants, and to eat and drink and be drunk, the master of that servant will come on a day when he is not looking for him, and at an hour when he is not aware, and will cut him in two and appoint him his portion with the unbelievers. And that servant who knew his master's will, and did not prepare himself or do according to his will, shall be beaten with many stripes. But he who did not know, yet committed things deserving of stripes, shall be beaten with few. For everyone to whom much is given, from him much will be required; and to whom much has been committed, of him they will ask the more (Luke 12:42-48).

God takes appropriation (stewardship) very seriously. We must do the same.

PILLAR #4: PRESERVATION

The fourth and final pillar of true wealth is wealth preservation. I said earlier that true wealth consists of things of lasting or even eternal value that never fade away, can perpetuate themselves, and are never subject to loss or reversal. This is preservation of wealth. In the financial realm this is called passive income: those assets and instruments that produce income automatically apart from working to earn a paycheck, thus continually building wealth. Jesus described the same concept in the spiritual realm when He said:

> *Do not lay up for yourselves treasures on earth, where moth and rust destroy and where thieves break in and steal; but lay up for yourselves treasures in heaven, where neither moth nor rust destroys and where thieves do not break in and steal. For where your treasure is, there your heart will be also* (Matthew 6:19-21).

Wise appropriation of our allocation is key to entering the next phase of wealth preservation. Once again we turn to Jesus' parable of the talents to illustrate this:

> *After a long time the lord of those servants came and settled accounts with them. So he who had received five talents came and brought five other talents, saying, "Lord, you delivered to me five talents; look, I have gained five more talents besides them." His lord said to him, "Well done, good and faithful servant; you were faithful over a few things, I will make you ruler over many things. Enter into the joy of your lord." He also who had received two talents came and said, "Lord, you delivered to me two talents; look, I have gained two more talents besides them." His lord said to him,*

"Well done, good and faithful servant; you have been faithful over a few things, I will make you ruler over many things. Enter into the joy of your lord." Then he who had received the one talent came and said, "Lord, I knew you to be a hard man, reaping where you have not sown, and gathering where you have not scattered seed. And I was afraid, and went and hid your talent in the ground. Look, there you have what is yours." But his lord answered and said to him, "You wicked and lazy servant, you knew that I reap where I have not sown, and gather where I have not scattered seed. So you ought to have deposited my money with the bankers, and at my coming I would have received back my own with interest. Therefore take the talent from him, and give it to him who has ten talents. For to everyone who has, more will be given, and he will have abundance; but from him who does not have, even what he has will be taken away. And cast the unprofitable servant into the outer darkness. There will be weeping and gnashing of teeth" (Matthew 25:19-30).

When the master returned from his journey and called his three servants to account, he praised the first two for their wise and faithful appropriation of what he had allocated to them. Because they were prepared, in position, and understood the four pillars of true wealth, they were entrusted with greater allocations and ushered into a higher dimension of abundance. The third servant, on the other hand, received not praise but condemnation from his master.

Rather than rising to greater things, he lost the allocation he had been given. He experienced no wealth preservation because he failed to understand or appreciate the four pillars of true wealth.

Although this parable of the servants involves the allocation of money, the principle applies universally to every area of life. Whether in the things of the earth or the things of the Spirit, if you want to rise to greater heights, you first must prove yourself wise and faithful where you are with what you have. You must show yourself trustworthy in small things before God will trust you with bigger things. This is true whether we are talking about money, work, career, school, church, home, influence, power, or anything else. As the old saying goes, "Bloom where you are planted." If you truly want to be a light to the world, first make sure that you are faithful being a light in your community, in your neighborhood, on your own street, and in your own house.

If you want to be poor no more, remember that there are no paupers in the Kingdom of heaven. Be faithful where you are with what you have, trust the Lord and follow Him, and He will raise you up into your shining destiny as a radiant light in a dark world with wealth—true wealth—beyond your wildest dreams.

Chapter Nine

POOR NO MORE

The future belongs to the children of God. It always has. This sounds counterintuitive because, by all appearances, those who ignore God and pursue wealth, power, position, and influence hold all the advantages. The world seems to be going its way while Christians are shunted to the sidelines and the church is deemed irrelevant and completely out of fashion. Many people today, particularly in the West, feel that the church and the Christian "religion" have nothing to offer them; Christianity is simply a leftover of an earlier, simpler, and more naive age.

Appearances can be deceiving, however. The Bible presents a very different picture from that of the world as to who will triumph and prevail in the end. Although the world adulates the rich and powerful, the Bible says that it is the meek (gentle) who will inherit the earth (Matt. 5:5). Although the world aspires to happiness in the pursuit of material wealth and physical pleasures, the Bible says that it is those who hunger and thirst after righteousness who will be satisfied (Matt. 5:6). Although the world admires those who employ cutthroat, winner-take-all strategies in their rise to the top, the Bible says that it is the merciful who shall obtain mercy (Matt. 5:7). And although ungodly people and institutions seem to control most of the world's wealth, the Bible says that *"the wealth of the sinner is stored up for the righteous"* (Prov. 13:22b).

In other words, despite appearances to the contrary, the children of God will inherit the new heaven and the new earth while those who reject God will be cast out:

> *Now I saw a new heaven and a new earth, for the first heaven and the first earth had passed away. Also there was no more sea. Then I, John, saw the holy city, New Jerusalem, coming down out of heaven from God, prepared as a bride adorned for her husband. And I heard a loud voice from heaven saying, "Behold, the tabernacle of God is with men, and He will dwell with them, and they shall be His people. God Himself will be with them and be their God. And God will wipe away every tear from their eyes; there shall be no more death, nor sorrow, nor crying. There shall be no more pain, for the former things have passed away." Then He who sat on the throne said, "Behold, I make all things new." And He said to me, "Write, for these words are true and faithful." And He said to me, "It is done! I am the Alpha and the Omega, the Beginning and the End. I will give of the fountain of the water of life freely to him who thirsts. He who overcomes shall*

inherit all things, and I will be his God and he shall be My son. But the cowardly, unbelieving, abominable, murderers, sexually immoral, sorcerers, idolaters, and all liars shall have their part in the lake which burns with fire and brimstone, which is the second death" (Revelation 21:1-8).

A great shift is coming in the world order. Power, authority, wealth, and influence will be transferred from the unrighteous to the people of God, those who have been oppressed, repressed, rejected, dismissed, ignored, marginalized, and victimized by the world. Jesus Himself was *"despised and rejected by men, a Man of sorrows and acquainted with grief"* (Is. 53:3a), so it is not surprising that the same lot would befall those who follow Him. In fact, Jesus made it clear that such would be the case:

If the world hates you, you know that it hated Me before it hated you. If you were of the world, the world would love its own. Yet because you are not of the world, but I chose you out of the world, therefore the world hates you. Remember the word that I said to you, "A servant is not greater than his master." If they persecuted Me, they will also persecute you. If they kept My word, they will keep yours also. But all these things they will do to you for My name's sake, because they do not know Him who sent Me (John 15:18-21).

The troubles and sorrows we experience in this life as children of God—and they are many—are limited to this life; they will be gone in the life to come. Jesus said, *"These things I have spoken to you, that in Me you may have peace. In the world you will have tribulation; but be of good cheer, I have overcome the world"* (John 16:33). Just as Jesus suffered in this world, so will we as His followers. And just as Jesus overcame the world, in Him we too shall overcome.

Every person who has been born again of the Spirit of God through faith in Jesus Christ will inherit the Kingdom of heaven. But not every believer will be given equal blessings, responsibilities, and leadership in the new order. The greatest transference will come to those who not only know the Lord by faith but who also are totally sold out to Him and committed to His Kingdom agenda. God will not transfer power, wealth, and leadership in His Kingdom to people who lack spiritual discipline or whose thoughts are consumed by greed, arrogance, or self-aggrandizement. He has reserved the transference of His Kingdom assets to those of His children who have prepared and positioned themselves and surrendered their lives to the tenets, authority, and leadership of the Holy Spirit.

HOW TO POSITION YOURSELF FOR THE KINGDOM

This transference, then, will be selective and will come only to those believers who have:

1. Focused their hearts on God's *agenda.*
2. Disciplined their minds to God's *attitude.*
3. Positioned themselves to receive God's *assets.*

None of this happens automatically. If your desire is to be one of those select few whom God chooses to bless with such transference, you will have to adjust your life in several significant ways. First, you will have to make a paradigm shift. A paradigm is a pattern or model that shapes the way you look at the world. Your background, upbringing, education, and experiences all play a part in constructing your particular paradigm, the "lens" through which you view the world. A paradigm shift, then, is a fundamental change in your approach and mind-set. If you want to receive transference, you have to shift your paradigm. You have to position yourself to be on God's agenda, which means being willing to change or even abandon your own agenda, change your psyche, and change the way you think.

Every person in the Bible who encountered God was faced with a paradigm shift. Some of them made that shift; many did not. When Moses, a fugitive murderer in self-imposed exile in the desert, encountered God in the burning bush, he had to shift his paradigm to accept God's agenda of him being the one chosen to lead the Israelites out of slavery in Egypt. When Jesus' disciples finally came to the understanding that He was the Son of God and the Messiah, they had to shift from their paradigm of expecting Jesus to be a political savior who would liberate them from Rome and reestablish Israel as a glorious earthly kingdom to a new paradigm of understanding that His mission was to announce the coming of the Kingdom of God and to die for the sins of all people. When the rich young ruler asked Jesus what he needed to do to receive eternal life, he faced a paradigm shift when Jesus told him to sell everything he had, give to the poor, and follow Him. In this case, the man proved unwilling to change his paradigm. Instead of adjusting himself to Jesus' agenda, he went away sorrowful.

You can't keep thinking the way you think at your current level if you want to rise to a higher level. God is calling you to a higher level, but you will have to shift your paradigm from your agenda to His.

The second way you will have to adjust your life to receive transference is to commit yourself to a lifestyle of radical obedience to God. You have to be in compliance with God's orders for your life; you must be totally submissive to His will. Whatever God tells you to do, do it without hesitation or delay. Get your obedience in order; cultivate the obedient heart of a willing servant. God never blesses in the midst of disobedience. He will not entrust His treasures to people who are focused on their own desires and who do not wait on Him or listen to His voice. The Bible says that obedience is better than sacrifice, so examine your obedience factor carefully.

GOD IS CALLING YOU TO A HIGHER LEVEL.

A third adjustment you will have to make is in your prayer life. People who are in position to receive transference are people who are deeply committed to prayer. A quick blessing before every meal or an occasional perfunctory prayer is not enough. You must cultivate a deep, rich, and intimate fellowship with God through prayer. He deeply desires such a relationship with you, and, indeed, with all of us.

Finally, you will have to adjust your life to the constant pursuit of wisdom. Proverbs 9:10 says, *"The fear of the Lord is the beginning of wisdom, and the knowledge of the Holy One is understanding."* If you need wisdom, all you have to do is ask: *"If any of you lacks wisdom, let him ask of God, who gives to all liberally and without reproach, and it will be given to him"* (James 1:5). You need to become like the sons of Issachar, *"who had understanding of the times"* (1 Chron. 12:32). Understanding the times requires wisdom, and wisdom comes from the Lord.

We find these four life adjustments on display in the lives of many characters throughout the Bible. I have already mentioned Moses, who went through a paradigm shift at the burning bush and was transformed from an obscure shepherd in exile to the deliverer of a nation. With his paradigm shift came a shift in everything else. Once he accepted God's call, Moses became God's man completely, walking in thorough obedience that resulted in numerous miracles being performed through him. Moses also became such a man of prayer that he enjoyed an intimate, face-to-face relationship with God unrivaled by anyone else in the Bible except Jesus Himself. And because of this close fellowship, Moses exercised great wisdom. Moses received a transference.

Joseph is another example. Sold into slavery in Egypt by his jealous brothers and later imprisoned under false charges, Joseph endured years of obscurity until the day God elevated him to power in Egypt, second only to Pharaoh. Joseph adjusted his paradigm to fit every situation, from freedom to slavery to imprisonment to promotion, maintaining a firm faith in God through it all. He also was faithful in his obedience to God, never surrendering his principles or his integrity simply to improve his own situation. He was undoubtedly a man of prayer, and his close walk with God resulted in great wisdom, which he demonstrated when he interpreted Pharaoh's dream of the coming famine. Impressed, Pharaoh promoted Joseph to a position of power so he could deal with the crisis. Joseph received a transference.

David, a man after God's own heart, also began in obscurity. The youngest son of his father, David spent his early years in the fields, shepherding his family's flocks. He probably would have stayed there, too, had God not chosen him to be king of Israel. From shepherd to king is quite a paradigm shift, but David adjusted successfully because his heart was focused on God and he had an obedient spirit. The powerful psalms that he penned prove that he was a mighty man of prayer, and his reign as king was, for the most part, characterized by wisdom exceeded only by his son and successor, Solomon. David received a transference.

Daniel, likewise, rose from anonymity to prominence. Taken into captivity in Babylonia from his home in Judah, Daniel had to shift his paradigm from freedom to a life in exile. Because of his steadfast obedience to God and his faithfulness in prayer, Daniel became the wisest of all the wise men who served in the court of the Babylonian king. Daniel received a transference.

One characteristic that all four of these men shared in common is that God brought them from obscurity to prominence. And because they all demonstrated the four characteristics of obedience, prayer, wisdom, and the ability to shift their paradigm, they each received a transference from God that elevated them to the place where they could fulfill their destiny in God's plan. In seasons of transfer God brings people from obscure places and elevates them to positions of influence and renown. He is always grooming champions in the backside of the wilderness, preparing and seasoning them in anonymity until that day arrives for them to be revealed. If you pay the price to prepare yourself to receive transference, God will do the same for you. He will bless you in the midst of unsaved people. He will elevate you for godly influence in the midst of an ungodly world. He will raise you up as a bright beacon of hope in the midst of darkness.

> GOD IS ALWAYS GROOMING CHAMPIONS IN THE BACKSIDE OF THE WILDERNESS.

DEVELOPING GODLY CHARACTER

When God gets ready to give transference, He looks for people of godly character and mind-set. This is why I said you have to be focused on God's agenda, disciplined to God's attitude, and positioned to receive His assets. You have to be willing to shift your paradigm, walk in obedience to God, be fervent in prayer, and always seek wisdom. All of these are critical to the development of godly character. But there are a few other elements you need as well.

The first of these is *faith*. Faith is central to everything. Hebrews 11:6 says that it is impossible to please God without faith. Faith is the key that ultimately will shift your whole situation. The apostle Paul said that faith comes by hearing, and hearing by the Word of God (Rom. 10:17). Hearing the Word refers to preaching, but it can also refer to any other method of getting God's Word into your heart and mind, such as by reading and studying it regularly. If you want to grow your faith, develop the habit of getting into the Word of God every day. You cannot expect transference or expect to prosper in God's Kingdom economy if you lack faith. Where faith is lacking, fear steps in. Faith liberates but fear paralyzes. Faith will take you where you want to go but fear will trap you where you are.

The Bible is the living Word of God, and it will build faith in those who read it with serious purpose. Here are a couple of examples:

So Jesus answered and said to them, "Have faith in God. For assuredly, I say to you, whoever says to this mountain, 'Be removed and be cast into the sea,' and does not doubt in his heart, but believes that those things he says will be done, he will have whatever he says. Therefore I say to you, whatever things you ask when you pray, believe that you receive them, and you will have them" (Mark 11:22-24).

And God is able to make all grace abound toward you, that you, always having all sufficiency in all things, may have an abundance for every good work (2 Corinthians 9:8).

At all times, and especially during this season of transference, it is vitally important to build your faith by reading God's Word regularly, believing what it says, and backing up your belief with obedience.

Another critical element for developing godly character is *contentment*. Only when you have learned to be content with what you have, only when you have freed yourself from the *obsession* for material wealth and possessions, can you be entrusted with true wealth assets of God. Paul expressed the proper attitude when he wrote:

Not that I speak in regard to need, for I have learned in whatever state I am, to be content: I know how to be abased, and I know how to abound. Everywhere and in all things I have learned both to be full and to be hungry, both to abound and to suffer need. I can do all things through Christ who strengthens me (Philippians 4:11-13).

The Book of Proverbs also contains wisdom regarding contentment:

Two things I request of You (deprive me not before I die): Remove falsehood and lies far from me; give me neither poverty nor riches—feed me with the food allotted to me; lest I be full and deny You, and say, "Who is the Lord?" Or lest I be poor and steal, and profane the name of my God (Proverbs 30:7-9).

Contentment is a guardian against greed, which is deadly and will destroy everyone who is enslaved by it. Proverbs 15:27 says, *"He who is greedy for gain troubles his own house, but he who hates bribes will live."* None of us are immune to the spirit of greed. We must guard against it constantly, and one of our best weapons is cultivating an attitude of contentment. Greed is a consuming lust that never rests, while contentment fosters peace.

The world is full of greedy people, and unfortunately, many of them are found in the church. Greedy people are like little children who are always shouting, "It's mine! It's mine!" No matter how much they have, it is never enough, and they are too busy focusing on themselves to think about anyone else. Psalm 37:4 says, *"Delight yourself also in the Lord, and He shall give you the desires of your heart."* Think about that for a moment. If you delight yourself in the Lord, He will be the greatest desire of your heart! So the key to contentment is to *"love the Lord your God with all your heart, with all your soul, and with all your strength"* (Deut. 6:5). This too may be a paradigm shift for you. If the Lord God is the supreme love of your life, nothing else can get a foothold to capture your heart, and, like Paul, you can learn to be content no matter what your situation.

A third characteristic of godly character is *integrity*. To have integrity means to be complete or undivided, particularly in the sense of being consistent in both your words and your actions. Integrity means adhering steadfastly to the highest principles and standards of moral and ethical behavior. Proverbs 20:7 says, *"The righteous man walks in his integrity; his children are blessed after him."* Living with integrity brings blessings that extend to successive generations. Proverbs 22:1 says, *"A good name is to be chosen rather than great riches, loving favor rather than silver and gold."* People of integrity never sell out their standards or compromise their principles for any reason, not even for personal gain. They understand that if you sacrifice your integrity, you lose everything. Integrity and honesty are the two calling cards in God's Kingdom economy. When you possess these ingredients, they open a door for you to position yourself for unlimited access to God's assets. Remember that your motive in desiring God's assets is to pursue His agenda, not yours. This too is what it means to have integrity.

By many outward appearances, we live in a topsy-turvy world. Our hearts tell us that good people should prosper and get ahead while evil people struggle and fail, but the reality we see around us often seems to show the opposite. Evil people, immoral people, dishonest and unethical people, and people who have no concern for God and His ways quite often appear to have everything going for them while the children of God struggle from day to day. This apparent injustice, where evil people prosper and good people suffer, is an age-old problem; as the writer of Ecclesiastes said, there really is nothing new under the sun. One ancient Hebrew poet who wrestled with this question expressed his feelings in a psalm:

Truly God is good to Israel, to such as are pure in heart. But as for me, my feet had almost stumbled; my steps had nearly slipped. For I was envious of the boastful, when I saw the prosperity of the wicked. For there are no pangs in their death, but their strength is firm. They are not in trouble as other men, nor are they plagued like other men.... Their eyes bulge with abundance; they have more than heart could wish. They scoff and speak wickedly concerning oppression; they speak loftily. They set their mouth against the heavens, and their tongue walks through the earth.... And they say, "How does God know? And is there knowledge in the Most High?" Behold, these are the ungodly, who are always at ease; they increase in riches. Surely I have cleansed my heart in vain, and washed my hands in innocence. For all day long I have been plagued, and chastened every morning.... When I thought how to understand this, it was too painful for me—until I went into the sanctuary of God; then I understood their end. Surely You set them in slippery places; You cast them down to destruction. Oh, how they are brought to desolation, as in a moment! They are utterly consumed with terrors (Psalm 73:1-5,7-9,11-14,16-19).

As this psalm illustrates, the apparent success and prosperity of the wicked is only an illusion. Despite their seeming invincibility, their eventual downfall is certain. The day is coming when the Lord of righteousness will set right everything that is wrong and vindicate His people. Transference is coming for those of God's people who are prepared, positioned, and ready to receive it. Will you be one of them? Focus your heart on God's agenda. Discipline your mind to hold His attitude. Position yourself to receive His assets. Shift your thinking to God's paradigm. Commit yourself to a life of radical obedience to God. Resolve to become a prayer warrior. Pursue wisdom above riches through a holy fear of the Lord. Build your faith through regular interaction with the Word of God. Cultivate a heart of contentment by learning to delight yourself in the Lord above all else. Walk in integrity, complete and undivided, standing firm in honor and in your moral and ethical principles, even if you have to stand alone. None of this will happen overnight; it will take time. But as

> GOD'S ABUNDANCE IS A TREASURE GREATER THAN ANY AMOUNT OF GOLD.

you grow in these things in the power of the Holy Spirit, you will position yourself to receive God's transference. Then He will bless your life with abundance in every area, and that is a treasure greater than any amount of gold.

The opening verses of Psalm 37 contain some very precious promises for every believer who will walk the extra mile to pursue intimate fellowship with God and position him or herself to receive everything that God eagerly awaits to give:

> *Do not fret because of evildoers, nor be envious of the workers of iniquity. For they shall soon be cut down like the grass, and wither as the green herb. Trust in the Lord, and do good; dwell in the land, and feed on His faithfulness. Delight yourself also in the Lord, and He shall give you the desires of your heart. Commit your way to the Lord, trust also in Him, and He shall bring it to pass. He shall bring forth your righteousness as the light, and your justice as the noonday. Rest in the Lord, and wait patiently for Him; do not fret because of him who prospers in his way, because of the man who brings wicked schemes to pass. Cease from anger, and forsake wrath; do not fret—it only causes harm. For evildoers shall be cut off; but those who wait on the Lord, they shall inherit the earth. For yet a little while and the wicked shall be no more; indeed, you will look carefully for his place, but it shall be no more. But the meek shall inherit the earth, and shall delight themselves in the abundance of peace* (Psalm 37:1-11).

Chapter Ten

Make the Switch to Rich

It's time to make the switch to rich. A world of virtually unlimited possibilities awaits those who are willing to expend the time and effort to position themselves to receive the blessings and favor of God. If you have stayed with me this far in this book, then you may very well be one of those people. So I want to close out this study by sharing with you ten tips or keys to making the switch to rich. These ten keys will perform two functions. First, they will serve as a summary of sorts of what has gone before in the previous nine chapters. Second, they will serve as a handy quick reference guide that will help you focus your attention on the essentials and avoid getting sidetracked onto secondary issues. With these things in mind, then, let's get started.

1. LET GO OF YESTERDAY AND EMBRACE TOMORROW.

Let the past stay in the past. Don't allow guilt or regret over your past failures or sins hijack your future. Temporary failures are an inevitable part of life as well as essential stepping stones on the road to success. And temporary failures are just that—temporary. Don't allow a temporary failure or setback tie you down permanently. Failure can be a great teacher, so learn from your mistakes. Get up, dust yourself off, and keep going.

Your greatest days lie ahead of you. Successful people are always looking forward. The past is over and done, set and unchangeable. Since you cannot change the past, nothing is gained by lingering there. Blessings, success, and fulfillment come by embracing the future. Let the old things die away; fix your attention on the new day. After all, this is the biblical way. Second Corinthians 5:17 says, *"Therefore, if anyone is in Christ, he is a new creation; old things have passed away; behold, all things have become new."* God Himself said, "I *am* the God of Abraham, Isaac, and Jacob." He did not say, "I *was* the God of Abraham, Isaac, and Jacob." He redeemed your past so that you are free to move ahead into the bright future and

> YOUR GREATEST DAYS LIE AHEAD OF YOU.

glorious destiny that He has for you. What lies ahead? A *new* heaven and a *new* earth, ushered in by the One who says, *"Behold, I make all things new"* (Rev. 21:5).

Let go of yesterday. Let go of your guilt, your regrets, your failures, and your mistakes. Glean whatever is useful from these experiences and bring it with you; discard all the rest. Embrace the future with open arms, for that is where your destiny lies. When the Israelites were in exile in Babylonia because of their sins, God promised to deliver them from their captivity and restore them to their homeland:

> *For I know the thoughts that I think toward you, says the Lord, thoughts of peace and not of evil, to give you a future and a hope. Then you will call upon Me and go and pray to Me, and I will listen to you. And you will seek Me and find Me, when you search for Me with all your heart. I will be found by you, says the Lord, and I will bring you back from your captivity...* (Jeremiah 29:11-14).

Let God deliver you from the captivity of your past and liberate you into the freedom of your glorious future in Him.

2. FIND YOUR FOCUS.

One common characteristic shared by most successful people is that they know how to focus. Although they may have wide interests and enjoy many different things, they have zeroed in on the one or two that they do best and devote the bulk of their time and attention to them. They know that they will be most productive and find the most fulfillment by focusing on the things they do really well; things for which they possess the proper gifts and skills. True "renaissance men" are rare. History has afforded us only a very few people who truly mastered multiple disciplines and were exceptional in every endeavor they undertook. For most of us, attempting to do too many things will only dissipate our energy wastefully. Rather than being hailed as a renaissance man or woman, a more accurate description would be, "jack of all trades but master of none."

In other words, putting too many irons in the fire or having your finger in too many pies usually results in mediocrity rather than excellence. To focus means to fix your gaze on one thing so you can see it clearly, and this is impossible if you are always jumping around from one thing to another, to another, to another. You need to find your focus. What are you most interested in? What are you passionate about? What gets you out of bed every morning? What gifts or natural talents do you possess? What marketable skills have you acquired through education, circumstance, or experience? Resurrect your dreams—if you could be or do anything in the world, what would it be? What abilities and qualifications do you already have for pursuing your dream, and which ones do you still need to acquire? Pray to the Lord to guide you through His Spirit and to give you wisdom in finding your focus so that you can fulfill that destiny that God has planted in your heart.

3. Seize your moment.

I'm sure you have heard the old adage, "Good things come to those who wait." And there can be no doubt that patience is a virtue. For most good things in life, timing is critical. Removing a cake from the oven before it is done or letting it bake too long both produce the same result: an inedible cake. Success comes in pulling the cake out at just the right time. Often, it is the same in life. If you act too soon or wait too long, you may miss a valuable opportunity.

So timing is very important. However, there is another component to success that is just as important: preparation. With this in mind, I would like to modify the above adage and say, "Good things come to those who are prepared." Timing does not mean much if you are not prepared to recognize and seize your opportunity when it comes. Most people take a haphazard approach to life. They have no concrete goals, and since they do not know where they are going, they have no plan in place to take them anywhere. Opportunities pass them by not only because they are unprepared but also because they are not even looking in the first place.

Being prepared means knowing where you want to go and having a plan to get you there. If you know where you want to go and what you need to get there, you will be alert and watchful for opportunities that will help you move toward your goal. Preparation will help you seize your moment when it arrives. It also helps you avoid wasting time. Time is the only component in life that is irrecoverable when

161

it is lost. Lose money, you can make more; lose a house, you can buy another one; lose a car, you can replace it. Lose time, however, and it is gone forever.

Ecclesiastes 3:1 says, *"To everything there is a season, a time for every purpose under heaven."* Prepare yourself. There is a season, a time that is just right for you. Stay alert, watch for it, and when it comes, seize your moment. It may not come your way again.

4. WEALTH IS NOT SOLELY FINANCIAL.

Throughout this book I have stressed the fact that wealth involves much more than money and financial prosperity. One of the major shortcomings of the "prosperity gospel" as it has been preached in America is its tendency to identify the blessings and favor of God almost exclusively with material wealth, while virtually ignoring the many kinds of wealth that have nothing to do with money. This emphasis on the material flies in the face of biblical teachings that appear to be perfectly clear and unambiguous. Let me give three examples. First of all, Jesus said, *"No one can serve two masters; for either he will hate the one and love the other, or else he will be loyal to the one and despise the other. Ye cannot serve God and mammon"* (Matt. 6:24). "Mammon" means money and material wealth. On another occasion He warned, *"Take heed and beware of covetousness, for one's life does not consist in the abundance of the things he possesses"* (Luke 12:15). In the verses that immediately follow, Jesus ascribes the word *fool* to any person who *"lays up treasure for himself, and is not rich toward God"* (Luke 12:20-21).

Finally, Jesus clearly states that true wealth is defined in terms of our relationship with God:

> *Do not lay up for yourselves treasures on earth, where moth and rust destroy and where thieves break in and steal; but lay up for yourselves treasures in heaven, where neither moth nor rust destroys and where thieves do not break in and steal. For where your treasure is, there your heart will be also* (Matthew 6:19-21).

There is no greater wealth than to be rich toward God, and that kind of wealth cannot be measured in dollar signs. Cultivate your relationship with Father God and lay up for yourself heavenly treasures through prayer, Bible reading and study, and obedience to the Word and commands of the Lord. Spend one-on-one time with Him every day. Make it the highest priority of your life.

Build up your mental wealth by immersing yourself in good literature, art, and other media that nourish the mind. Paul said, *"Finally, brethren, whatever things are true, whatever things are noble, whatever things are just, whatever things are pure, whatever things are lovely, whatever things are of good report, if there is any virtue and if there is anything praiseworthy—meditate on these things"* (Phil. 4:8). Stop feeding yourself trash talk, filth, profanity, obscenity, and ungodly language and images that are so prevalent in our music, television programming, movies, and the Internet today. Let your imagination flow freely. Learn to appreciate and celebrate the mental gifts God has given you. Don't be afraid to think; our world needs more serious thinkers. There is nothing wrong with a faith that has intellectual muscle. God gave you a mind; use it.

Don't forget the wealth found in relationships with family and friends. Who can put a price on laughter, good cheer, encouragement, and support, or the richness of belonging and acceptance, of loving and of being loved? British poet John Donne wrote, "No man is an island entire of itself; every man is a piece of the continent, a part of the main." God created us for connectedness, to Him first of all, and then to family and friends. We need God and we need family, and in the meeting of these needs we find our greatest wealth. This is entirely in keeping the two greatest commandments as identified by Jesus:

> *"You shall love the Lord your God with all your heart, with all your soul, and with all your mind." This is the first and great commandment. And the second is like it: "You shall love your neighbor as yourself." On these two commandments hang all the Law and the Prophets* (Matthew 22:37-40).

So when you think of wealth, think of God first, family second, friends third, and finally, only after everything else, think of money.

5. FIND YOUR SPOT.

God has a special spot for you in His Kingdom plan, and that spot is the place of extreme blessings. But you cannot get to that spot by using the philosophies or methods of the world because the Kingdom of God operates under a different economy.

The key to being rich toward God is to walk in obedience to His commands. Obedience means humble submission to the will and purposes of God in your life. It means surrendering your self-will; giving up your right to yourself in favor of

> ### THE ROAD TO TRUE WEALTH IS THE ROAD OF SERVITUDE.

God's absolute claim on your life through Jesus Christ. In other words, as counterintuitive as it may seem, the road to true wealth, genuine success, and greatness in the Kingdom of God is the road of servitude. Jesus said, *"But he who is greatest among you shall be your servant"* (Matt. 23:11). He then demonstrated the truth of these words by living them out in His own behavior, especially by dying on the cross in obedience to His Father's will:

> *Let this mind be in you which was also in Christ Jesus, who, being in the form of God, did not consider it robbery to be equal with God, but made Himself of no reputation, taking the form of a bondservant, and coming in the likeness of men. And being found in appearance as a man, He humbled Himself and became obedient to the point of death, even the death of the cross. Therefore God also has highly exalted Him*

and given Him the name which is above every name,
that at the name of Jesus every knee should bow, of
those in heaven, and of those on earth, and of those
under the earth, and that every tongue should confess
that Jesus Christ is Lord, to the glory of God the Father
(Philippians 2:5-11).

Notice the progression. When the Son of God came to earth and took on human flesh, He *"made Himself of no reputation, taking the form of a **bondservant**."* That's the same thing as a slave. Then *"He humbled Himself and became obedient to the point of death."* Because of Jesus' humble submission to servitude and obedience, *"God... highly exalted Him and* [gave] *Him the name which is above every name."* First came humility, servitude, and obedience; then came exaltation, greatness, and blessings. First came surrender; then came prosperity.

Jesus has given us an example. There is no room for arrogance in God's Kingdom among God's people. That spot of extreme blessings God has for you can only be reached on the road of service and surrender, always remembering that everything God gives you still belongs to Him. No matter how successful or materially wealthy you may become, God still owns everything you have, and you are accountable to Him for its use. You are a steward, not an owner. Use well the resources He has entrusted to you, and He will entrust you with more. Extreme blessings come only with extreme surrender. That's the deal.

6. WEALTH CREATION.

No one ever gets rich working for somebody else. This is a fundamental principle of wealth creation. No matter what your profession, education, or skill level, if you work for someone else as an employee, your wealth creation options are limited. Ultimately, your employer controls your ability to create wealth because he determines how much he is willing to pay you. In many cases, of course, there is some flexibility for negotiation regarding salary, but in the end it boils down to what your employer is willing to pay and what you are willing to accept.

The clearest path to building personal wealth is to go into business for yourself. Although self-employment gets rid of the "middleman" of an employer where earnings are concerned, it is also not for the faint of heart. Most people are scared to death at the thought of going it on their own, much preferring the "security" of a steady job with a steady paycheck. Of course, any job is only as secure as the financial stability of the company, and the so-called "secure" job you have today could be gone tomorrow.

If the thought of supporting yourself and your family through your own business scares you, consider this fact: As a child of God you already have within you everything you need to create wealth and build a secure future for your loved ones. Deuteronomy 8:18 says, *"And you shall remember the Lord your God, for it is He who gives you power to get wealth, that He may establish His covenant which He swore to your fathers, as it is this day."* God has given you the power to create wealth; all you have to do is step out in faith and trust God to lead you. What marketable skills do you possess? What kind of business have you always dreamed of owning? What ideas or inventions have you thought of that could be developed to provide needed goods or services? Let your imagination soar. The key to your personal wealth and success is inside you right now. Ask God to reveal it to you and to give you the wisdom to use it.

7. WEALTH ACCUMULATION.

In order to accumulate wealth, at least two elements must be in place. First, your income must exceed your outgo. You must make more money than you spend. Stated another way, you must live within your means. It is impossible to accumulate wealth if you always spend every penny you make. In our consumer-focused and credit-driven economy we are encouraged to spend, spend, spend as if there is no tomorrow. And there *will* be no tomorrow, financially speaking, if you buy into that philosophy (no pun intended). In order to accumulate wealth, you must control your spending, minimize expenses, and eliminate personal debt. Careful budgeting may be needed in order to ensure that you have money left over to save, invest, and hold in reserve for emergencies.

The second element that must be present before you can accumulate wealth is the ability to look ahead, fixing your mind where you are going and how you are going to get there. This means that you must get rid of the mind-set of living only paycheck to paycheck. Develop the habit of taking some money from every paycheck and setting it aside to finance your future. Again, this can only happen if you are living within your means and have money left over after you have met all your legitimate expenses. Look to invest your funds in assets that have staying power, assets that do not lose their value, such as gold and real estate. As your assets permit, you may want to consider buying a franchise. Investing in the stock market is also a good strategy, but be careful how you invest and where you invest. Some investments are riskier than others but carry higher returns because of the higher risk. Never invest more than you can afford to lose, and never invest beyond your personal comfort zone regarding risk.

8. WEALTH ALLOCATION.

There is an old saying that you should never put all your eggs in the same basket. It makes sense. After all, one stumble, the basket falls, and you lose everything. This same principle applies when it comes to allocating your wealth. The financial term for this is *diversify.* Allocate your money to different areas of investments and into different financial vehicles. There are many options, and a competent financial counselor can help you determine the portfolio that best fits your temperament and your needs. Here are just a few: a money market account; certificates of deposit (CDs); U.S. government savings bonds; an IRA; mutual funds; trust funds; gold; oil; natural gas; and "green" energy such as wind and solar.

All investments carry a certain level of risk with corresponding rates of return. Low-risk investments are the ones where you are the least likely to lose your money, but the rate of return, while more certain, is lower than those of higher risk investments. Mid-risk and high-risk investments are more prone to loss than low-risk investments, but they offer substantially higher returns, which means if they pay off, you get much more "bang for your buck." Which level is best? That depends on the individual. However, a balanced portfolio containing an assortment of investment vehicles of each risk level is usually the wisest and most satisfactory approach. The idea behind diversification is to ensure that some of your investments are always making money for you even when some of the others are not.

9. WEALTH PRESERVATION.

Preserving your wealth for future generations depends on making the transition from active income to passive income. Active income is the money you make directly from your own work, either as wages or salary paid to you by an employer, or money you make from your own business. The problem with active income, however, particularly if it is your only source of income, is that if you become sick or disabled and cannot work, or if you lose your job, your income stops. What do you do then? Unless you have a financial reserve to carry you until you get well or find another job, you could find yourself in deep trouble very quickly. This is why it is so important to live within your means, eliminate your debt, minimize expenses, and set back money on a regular basis to plan for the future.

Passive income is income you will receive whether or not you are working. I'm not talking about welfare, food stamps, or unemployment benefits. I am talking about ongoing returns from investments you have made. This can take many forms: earned interest; royalties from books you have written; or from oil, gas, or mineral rights from properties you own; stock returns; cashing out certificates of deposit or savings bonds that have matured. The list could go on, but I think you get the idea. The whole point of passive income is to ensure the financial welfare of yourself and your loved ones without being dependent upon your continued ability to work and earn a paycheck. Active income is subject to the ups and downs of the economy, the job market, and your personal health. Passive income, on the other hand, is immune to these things. Passive income is recession-proof; it will be there regardless of the volatility of the economy and the uncertainties of daily life.

10. WEALTH APPRECIATION.

This is the time where you reflect upon God's goodness and mercy. You thank Him for the blessings He has poured out on you. A spirit of generosity swells within you and you have a passion to be a blessing to others. The time to do this is not way out there somewhere once you have "made it" (whatever that means). The time to do it is *now*. There is no minimum level of wealth or stability that you must reach before you can bless others or demonstrate generosity. Blessing begets blessing and generosity begets more blessing. Set your mind right now to bless others as you are blessed and to be generous in keeping up with your level of resources. Blessings and generosity depend not on your income level or your assets, but on the attitude of your heart. Second Corinthians 9:7 says that God loves a cheerful giver. The Greek word for "cheerful" literally means "hilarious." If you possess a cheerful or hilarious spirit toward giving, you can and will be generous regardless of your income level.

So establish the mind-set of thankfulness to God and generosity to others now, and let it grow in your spirit even as your wealth grows. Keep your eyes open because opportunities are all around you. As resources and opportunities allow, invest yourself and your means into church, people, missions, transitional homes, helping the homeless, feeding the hungry, ministering to the poor, the sick, and the needy, and a plethora of other philanthropic causes.

THE TIME TO BLESS OTHERS IS NOW.

The more you become involved in these types of ministries, the more you will become an agent of change. You will wake up every morning excited about the opportunities to make people, systems, and networks better. Blessing others as you have been blessed will become the joy of your life. You will become a living, walking testimony of Jesus Christ. Truly, you will have made the switch to rich.

About The Author

Kervin J. Smith is a skillful communicator, and one of the leading authorities in empowerment, increase, and biblical economics. He is a best selling author/conference speaker. His teaching and preaching is unique, scholarly, life-changing and relevant to everyday issues. There is a mandate on his life to break the chains of poverty over the lives of people throughout the world.

Dr. Kervin uses a holistic biblical approach to bring clarity and insight to people all over the world. He uses his background in the financial arena combined with biblical truth to bring clarity to people from all walks of life.

It is the writings and teachings of Dr. Kervin that inspire, motivate, and breathe life into dreams that were dead.

If you would like to schedule Dr. Kervin J. Smith for a speaking engagement contact:

Dr. Kervin J. Smith
P.O. Box 46401
Eden Prairie, MN 55344
E-mail: kervinjsmithmin@aol.com
Phone: (612) 408-0455

OTHER BOOKS BY THE AUTHOR

- Body Building: Getting the Church in Shape

- Jezebel's Church

- Living Single... The Different Faces of Singleness

- Prophetic Power

- When Women Talk, Men Should Listen

- Your Destiny Now!

- Overcoming the Enemy Within

- The Seven Spirits of A Woman (Fall 2012)